# The Texas Political System

*Dan Nimmo*
University of Missouri

*William Oden*
Texas Tech

Prentice-Hall, Inc.
Englewood Cliffs, New Jersey

© 1971 by Prentice-Hall, Inc., Englewood Cliffs, New Jersey

*All rights reserved. No part of this book may be reproduced in any form or by any means without permission in writing from the publisher.*

C-13-912477-2
P-13-912469-1

Library of Congress Catalog Card Number 72-146740
Printed in the United States of America

Current printing (last digit)
10 9 8 7 6 5 4 3 2 1

*Prentice-Hall International, Inc., London*
*Prentice-Hall of Australia, Pty. Ltd., Sydney*
*Prentice-Hall of Canada, Ltd., Toronto*
*Prentice-Hall of India Private Limited, New Delhi*
*Prentice-Hall of Japan, Inc., Tokyo*

# Contents

**PART ONE**
**TEXAS AND THE POLITICAL SETTING**

**1** TEXAS AS A POLITICAL SYSTEM 1 *Comparative State Political Systems* 2 *Social and political systems* 3 *The role participants, boundaries, and environments of state political systems* 6 *The Processes of State Political Systems* 10 *The input process* 10 *The output process* 12 *The conversion process* 13 *The Search for a Democratic Political System in Texas* 15

**2** THE ENVIRONMENT OF TEXAS POLITICS 19 *The Socioeconomic Environment of Texas Politics* 19 *The ethnic minorities of Texas* 20 *The changing economic background of Texas politics* 26 *The Constitutional Environment of Texas Politics* 33 *Political institutions in Texas* 33 *The contents of federalism and localism* 38

**PART TWO**
**POLITICAL INPUTS: ORGANIZING SUPPORTS AND DEMANDS IN TEXAS**

**3** MOBILIZING POLITICAL SUPPORTS 45 *Political Attitudes, Parties, and Participation in Texas* 46 *The political culture of Texas*

iii

*46 The Texas party system 54 Electoral participation in Texas 65 Support Politics in Texas 74*

**4** *PRESENTING POLITICAL DEMANDS 77 Interest Groups and Demand Politics 77 Interest groups in state political systems 78 Political interests in Texas 81 Techniques of Demand Politics 92 Institutionalizing privilege 93 Campaigning for candidates and policies 95 Lobbying for demands 97 Demand Politics in Texas 104*

# PART THREE
# POLITICAL OUTPUTS: POLICY-MAKING PROCESSES IN TEXAS

**5** *ORGANIZING THE CONVERSION PROCESS 107 The Conversion Process in Texas: Structure and Roles 107 The Gubernatorial Role: Initiator or Standpatter? 109 The executive authority of the governor 110 The legislative authority of the governor 112 The Legislative Role: Policy Deliberation in Texas Politics 118 The legislative system in Texas 118 Processes of legislative conversion 123 The Faceless Roles: Policy Application and Feedback 128 Administrative authority in Texas 128 Judicial authority in Texas 130 The Fragmented Organization of the Texas Conversion Process 131*

**6** *ALLOCATING COSTS AND BENEFITS 133 Varieties of Public Policies 134 Budgetary Outputs: Redistributive or Regulatory? 135 The allocation of benefits 137 The allocation of burdens 139 Economic Outputs: Further Regulatory Allocations 142 Reaction to Policy-Making: Support, Opposition, or Acquiescence? 145*

# PART FOUR
# A POSTSCRIPT

**7** *SYSTEM STABILITY AND CHANGE 149 Summary Aspects of Texas Politics 149 Implications of System Changes 152 The Patterns of Texas Democracy 154*

# Preface

In the last decade an increasing number of textbooks describing the government and politics of Texas has appeared. The reasons are not hard to fathom; namely, the fascination of Texas politics deserves scholarly comment, and the statutory requirement that all students in Texas public colleges and universities receive instruction in national and state government provides a built-in, captive readership. Indeed prospective readers of a newly published work—students, teachers, politicians, journalists, and others—rightfully demand that the authors justify adding another volume to the surfeit of existing works.

Curiously, perhaps, we contend that the very fact that so much has already been written about Texas government creates a place for this brief, interpretative work. Several excellent texts now describe the constitutional, social, political, administrative, and policy sides of Texas government. We seek not to add to the supply of these fine and detailed treatises, but to respond to a clear need generated by these comprehensive efforts—the need for a consistently applied framework within which readers can meaningfully analyze and evaluate the sometimes complex, often confusing, and always diverse range of Texas political phenomena. To this end we introduce and employ throughout our discussion a simplified version of a sophisticated tool of social inquiry: systems analysis. We do so in the conviction that a systems model is an extremely useful expository device in state politics. We do not ignore the topics that traditionally provide the grist for the mills of other

Texas government texts—social settings, geography, elections, political parties, pressure groups, gubernatorial-legislative relations, or administrative structures. Rather, we have endeavored to incorporate these aspects of Texas government into an internally consistent and constructively critical account of the Texas political system. We offer the finished product not as a definitive description but as a suggestive analysis, not as an exhaustive encyclopedia but as a concise interpretation.

A second rationale underlies the preparation of this textbook. The authors contend that a great deal of what has been written about Texas government ignores the fact that Texas is but one of many political systems in America. This has a two-fold impact. First, it implies that Texas is so unique as an entity as to be beyond comparison with other political systems. Second, that very uniqueness, when too strongly emphasized, leaves the impression that Texas politics are beyond comprehension by "non-Texans." As a result, the politics of few states are as inaccurately stereotyped, misunderstood, and misjudged by "outsiders" as the politics of Texas. Thus, although we too focus on the single system, we picture the state's politics within the larger context of other state systems and the federal system. We hope to represent fairly the uniqueness of Texas in a comparative fashion equally comprehensible to Texans and non-Texans alike.

Finally, researching this text we have attempted to ferret out published empirical studies that help to explain the nature of the Texas political system. But we have found that much of what passes for knowledge about Texas is based more on legend than research. In many areas no empirical data exists at all. Hence, we have been forced to raise more questions about the Texas political system than we have been able to supply answers. We fervently hope that this will not dismay readers. Indeed, we invite them to challenge our speculations by putting them to empirical test, and to answer our questions by becoming curious about and involved in Texas politics. Certainly no better justification for this or any other textbook could exist than that it stimulated sufficient interest and research to prove the authors *wrong*.

Although we as authors assume full responsibility for the success or failure of our approach, analysis, interpretation, and critique of the Texas political system, we wish to acknowledge the assistance of several individuals who contributed in various ways to this text's publication. Mr. James Murray and Mr. James Campbell provided ideas at an early stage, resulting in our efforts to adopt a novel approach to the description of state politics. Mr. David Grady followed the project and offered several helpful suggestions along the way. We wish to thank Professor Roy Meek of Colorado State University for his critical comments on portions of the manuscript. Professor David Welborn of Kansas University, a native Texan whose roots are still deeply embedded in Lamar County, read the manuscript with a critical outlook. Mr. Michael Hutchinson was helpful in gathering data concerning

Texas voting patterns. Mr. Blair Weir contributed his talents at computer programming. Mr. Roger Emblen and Miss Joan Brooks of Prentice-Hall, Inc., provided invaluable assistance in keeping the entire project on schedule.

# TEXAS AND THE POLITICAL SETTING

*PART ONE*

# 1

# Texas as a Political System

*Texas is the most cussed and discussed, demeaned and explained, celebrated and orated state in the Union. Much effort has been spent to rationalize why Texans are what they are—or to decide what it is exactly that they are.*[1]

For Texans in the 1970s the above statement, penned in the 1950s, is still very accurate. Following a controversial five years (1963-1968) in which a Texan was President of the Union, the peculiarities of Texas came even more sharply into focus. Out of the cussing and discussing, demeaning and explaining, celebration and oration, rationalizing and interpretation emerged some interesting myths about Texas politics. Strangely enough, few have ever been put to the test. It is not our intent to examine all of them here; nor, we hope, will we add to the growing body of Texas political folklore. We do propose, however, to take the next step in clarifying the nature of Texas government and politics: to establish a framework within which to describe and interpret Texas politics both in its uniqueness and its similarity to other governments, state and national. In short, our emphasis is as much upon Texas as a state of the Union as upon Texas as a state of mind.

In addition to our desire to provide readers with a framework for interpretations of Texas politics, we have ancillary purposes that should be

---

[1]Max Lerner, *America as a Civilization* (New York: Simon and Schuster, Inc., 1957), p. 200.

explicit. First, we shall put the Texas political system in perspective, comparing and contrasting it with the patterns and variations of other states and, hopefully, suggest some reasons for the similarities and differences. Second, however, we shall learn that we know relatively few of the things we really need to know to explain Texas politics. This ignorance exists because little research has systematically explored the behavior of Texas politicians and citizens. It has always been easier to turn to folklore than to fact. Where possible we shall draw upon existing research; more often we shall point to areas that demand investigation. Finally, we shall evaluate Texas as a democratic political system, asking in a time when there are growing demands for participatory democracy in American life from majorities and minorities of left, right, and center, "How does Texas measure up?"

## COMPARATIVE STATE POLITICAL SYSTEMS: THE TEXAS CASE

In looking at the politics of any state such as Texas we are faced with a huge number of activities—an election, a civics lecture in a high school, a demonstration on the steps of the state capitol, or perhaps a liquor still in the backwoods—each of which may be important in the overall scheme of government. Unless we have some way of sorting the important from the trivial, however, we can act only as the proverbial blind men attempting to describe an elephant by touching various parts of its anatomy. In the process we run the risk of mistaking our elephant for a fig tree, a snake, or a water hose. What we need is a pair of glasses to aid our perspective, one that will assist us to separate essentials from nonessentials, myths from realities.

In the systematic exploration of politics such glasses consist of a conceptual framework—the elementary terms, ideas, and assumptions that guide us in selecting and interpreting facts. Many such frameworks are available to students of state politics. Political scientists call the framework we shall employ *systems analysis*. It is an approach that scientists have found helpful in studying various types of human behavior. It depicts physical, biological, and social behavior—individual and collective—as responses to environmental stimuli; both the stimuli and the internal makeup of the system influence the character of the responses. Although scholars differ over various nuances of the approach, there is consensus on the essentials of systems analysis. Let us look at each of these fundamentals.[2]

---

[2]Walter Buckley, ed., *Modern Systems Research for the Behavioral Scientist* (Chicago: Aldine Publishing Company, 1968).

## SOCIAL AND POLITICAL SYSTEMS

Any *system* consists of two or more elements that interact with one another; thus, a change in one element is accompanied by a change in the others, and the interaction of all elements forms a pattern of mutually interdependent parts. To understand the character of a particular element we must describe it as a part of the whole.[3] For example, a container of gas is a system; changes in the movements of some gas molecules (produced by applying heat) affect the movements of others with a resulting change in the volume and pressure of the gas. Blood circulates in the human body through a system of arteries, veins, and the heart; a hardening of the arteries means added effort for the heart to pump blood. Finally, think of the transaction between the buyer and seller of a commodity. In the exchange between the two components of the system the buyer gives up money but comes away with the product; the seller no longer has the commodity, but has increased his money.

Society can be viewed in a similar fashion as a pattern of interacting units. A *social system* consists of two or more persons interacting in a relatively persistent, patterned relationship, in which a change in the behavior of one person or group affects the others.[4] In a game of poker, for example, what one player does with his cards affects the decisions and options of his opponents; similarly the expressions of one committee member in a meeting occupy the time and attention of other members.

Students of human behavior contend that for social systems to persist certain requirements must be met. First, any social system exists within a particular environment; that is, lying outside the boundaries of the interactions making up the system are influences constantly brought to bear on interacting members. The system must react and adjust to these environmental influences. In our friendly poker contest the players must adapt the behavior to such possibilities as the impatience of wives at late arrivals home, an inability to function well the next day if the game does not break up early, or a depletion of funds.

Second, members of a social system must decide what goals they seek and mobilize their resources to attain them. Do the poker players want to get home early, insure that each member "breaks even," use the game as an excuse for getting away from home, or consume large quantities of food and drink? The ends sought affect the play of the game or the character of the system.

---

[3]Abraham Kaplan, *The Conduct of Inquiry* (San Francisco: Chandler Publishing Company, 1964), p. 333.
[4]Talcott Parsons, *The Social System* (New York: The Free Press, 1951), pp. 3-23; William C. Mitchell, *Sociological Analysis and Politics* (Englewood Cliffs, N. J.: Prentice-Hall, Inc., 1967).

Third, a social system must integrate its members into the whole sufficiently so that the system is not constantly in danger of breaking down. Since the actions of members are interdependent, the removal of one or more members could destroy the system. Integration occurs through continuing successful attempts to forge agreements on goals, rules of procedure, and lines of authority. In our poker game there must be some agreement as to how much may be wagered on a given play of the cards and who has the authority to rule what cards a player must have to open betting.

Finally, closely related to the problem of integration through consensus on goals, rules, and controls is the requirement that system members agree upon behavior for resolving disputes that does not destroy the system. In poker it is simply "understood" that in a "friendly" game a loser accepts his loss without threatening the lives of winners. But if the system's members have not learned to respect one another's lives, there is always the threat that one or more of them may take it upon himself to wage war against the others. In most social systems accepted standards of conduct are normally transmitted from generation to generation through the family, school, and other institutions.

A social system, then, is a set of interactions of mutually interdependent people. Its continued existence depends upon the members' capacity to adjust adequately to environmental influences, decide upon goals and mobilize resources to attain them, integrate themselves into the system, and maintain a minimal consensus on values and ways of behaving. But our concern is not with social systems as such but with a particular aspect, or subsystem, of society: the political system, or polity. Within the framework of the social system what are the major features and functions of politics?

When we say that politics is a subsystem we imply that its essential features are the same as those of any system (interacting units in a patterned relationship) but that the polity (political system) is only a single set of the multiple interactions—economic, religious, friendship, marital, etc.—that comprise the social system. These other subsystems are a major source of the environmental influences on the polity: changes in one of these interdependent units effect changes in others. This interdependence places the polity under continuing stress to respond to the environmental influences from other social subsystems. We label these *inputs* and the political system's responses *outputs*.

We said earlier that for a social system to persist in the face of changes in its environment, its members must decide upon their collective goals, mobilize resources to attain them, and maintain the authority to unite members behind these aims and decisions. But within a society there are usually conflicting views about the allocation of resources—that is, who should benefit and who should suffer. For example, witness American society following man's first successful landing on the moon in July, 1969. Minutes after the venture some demanded that the nation commit its resources to landing on Mars; others insisted that the energy be turned to a massive effort to relieve poverty and hunger on Earth.

When disputes arise over goals, resource mobilization and allocation, and benefits and deprivations, how are they to be settled? Their resolution is the special province of the *political system*: that set of interactions which regulates conflicting demands within society by making authoritative policies (policies accepted by society's members as binding) about goals, resources, and benefits and costs.[5] Hence, the political subsystem possesses the authority that enables the social system to persist.

In America we have several sets of governing authorities. At the national level political interactions revolve around the written and unwritten provisions of the U.S. Constitution—these comprise the federal government, or subsystem. At another level are 50 separate, autonomous state governments. Each consists of a set of activities, a subsystem, interacting with the federal subsystem. To cite one case, in 1970 Texas received $38 million for its public schools under a federal law alloting monies for partial costs of educating children whose parents work or live on federal installations exempt from local taxation. State subsystems also interact with one another (Texas politicians, for instance, once proposed a plan to import water from the Mississippi river across Arkansas and Louisiana; voters defeated it in 1969), and are linked with myriad local political arrangements in cities, counties, villages, and special districts. (For example, the capacity of Texas cities to raise revenue to respond to local problems is severely restricted by policies made in Austin.) Viewed individually, each polity at the national, state, and local level is a political system in its own right regulating the conflicting demands from its particular environment. Viewed collectively, however, all polities interlock—disturbing and responding to one another—in intricate interactions that define the total American polity. Finally, to add to the complexity, all of these governing authorities possess institutions—legislatures, executives, bureaucracies, courts, political parties, pressure groups, election patterns—which have system characteristics of their own.

However, we do not center our attention here upon the total American polity.[6] We are interested instead in one part of it, which we shall treat as a

---

[5]David Easton, *A Systems Analysis of Political Life* (New York: John Wiley and Sons, 1965), p. 21; William C. Mitchell, *The American Polity* (New York: The Free Press, 1962).

[6]Systems analysis is certainly appropriate for examining other polities than the American. See, for example, H. V. Wiseman, *Political Systems* (New York: Frederick A. Praeger, 1966) and Morton A. Kaplan, *System and Process in International Politics* (New York: John Wiley & Sons, Inc., 1957).

single political system regulating conflicts within its social environment. To see how Texas government approaches the model of the state political system introduced thus far let us look more closely at that model by considering the following:

1. Who are the participants in and what are the boundaries and environments of state political systems such as Texas?
2. How are conflicting social demands presented as inputs to state political systems?
3. How are resolutions of conflicts fed back into the environments of state political systems as outputs?
4. How are inputs converted to outputs in state politics, and most significantly, who controls this process and to whose advantage?

## THE ROLE PARTICIPANTS, BOUNDARIES, AND ENVIRONMENTS OF STATE POLITICAL SYSTEMS

The character of a system is determined in large measure by the type of interacting units in it. Thus, a solar system consists of planets, satellites, and heat sources; an automotive system is made up carburetors, accelerators, etc. The basic units of a social system are, of course, interacting people, but systems analysis is not concerned with total personalities but with the behavior of persons in specific roles. By *role* we mean the segment of behavior of an individual that responds to the acts of others in a system. That role is shaped by how the individual thinks he should behave in a particular situation and the fashion in which other members think he should behave. In a marital system, for example, a man and woman perform the roles of husband and wife, and each expects the other to act in certain ways. But, at his work the man performs another role, say that of a realtor, with a far different set of expectations attached to it.

What, then, are the roles in a political system? Basically we can designate any behavior related to the polity's essential function—the authoritative regulation of social conflict—as a political role. We are particularly interested in identifying Texas' *gatekeepers*; that is, the individuals or groups who play the most influential roles in the political system—who initiate demands, make crucial decisions, and mobilize public opinion for or against policy proposals. Several examples of roles are the Governor of Texas, a state legislator, a mayor, a lobbyist, and perhaps a political reporter. Many groups also perform political roles: the Texas Road Builders' Association, the Texas Democratic Party, the Political Association of Spanish-Speaking Organizations, or a local civic club. Moreover, various institutions obviously perform political roles—legislative committees, the Attorney General's office, the University of Texas, the Dallas *Morning News*, etc. In the chapters that follow it will be one of our major tasks to identify clearly the nature of the individual, group, party, and institutional participants performing political roles in Texas.

We have said that political systems have boundaries. For a state system such as Texas, the boundaries that separate it from other polities consist of geographical, legal, and practical political demarcations. Geographic boundaries enclose the area in which a state may perform its functions; it may not tax, build highways, or arrest people outside of them. The type of geographic boundaries a state has certainly influences its politics. The fact that Texas borders the Gulf of Mexico generates political demands related to shipping, port facilities, and off-shore searches for oil resources; its boundary with Mexico raises interesting questions concerning migrant workers and economic exchanges.

Legal boundaries for states are two-fold. First, the U.S. Constitution separates the states from the federal system by restraining the former from coining money, conducting foreign affairs, or raising armies. (The provisions of the Constitution are not always clear, however, and the relationship of federal and state subsystems has undergone considerable stress in matters of desegregation, welfare, and educational policy because of the vagueness.) Second, states have their own constitutions that separate individual states from one another and limit a state's authority in dealing with its social, educational, religious, and other systems. The Texas Constitution is notorious for the limits it places on governing officials (a matter we review in Chapter 2).

Practical political considerations also place boundaries on state systems. The day-to-day operation of local governing authorities within states simply cannot be supervised by the state government, the legal superior of towns, cities, and counties. Disputes erupt regularly between local and state officials requiring redrawing of the boundaries between the two authorities. At the same time the activities of the federal government—really a subsystem of the United States political system—increasingly impinge upon matters once the province only of the states. Whereas once states alone set safety standards for highways and automobiles, now they must have standards conforming to federal demands in order to receive much-needed funds for construction. The practical problems of politics in a complex age thus place state systems in a position of constantly attempting to protect the boundaries of their authority.[7]

The boundaries of a state system not only separate it from other polities, but also separate the state polity from its internal environment. From that environment flow the conflicting demands that the polity must balance

---

[7]Herbert Jacob, "State Political Systems," in Herbert Jacob and Kenneth N. Vines, eds., *Politics in the American States* (Boston: Little, Brown & Co., 1965), pp. 16-18.

to assure a minimal consensus on goals, mobilization of resources, and allocation of benefits and costs. The environments of state political systems have at least five dimensions—the physical, social, economic, constitutional, and cultural. We describe the environment of the Texas political system more specifically in Chapters 2 and 3.

The physical environment of state systems affects politics in several ways. First, the natural resources of a state determine its capacity to respond to diverse demands. If a state can tax gas, oil, bauxite, or coal producers, for example, it may not need to burden its citizens with high income taxes. Second, physical features determine where people live. For example, prior to the 1940s settlement in far West Texas was relatively sparse, but with the advent of deep well irrigation the land became more attractive and the area has undergone a population boom. Similarly, Houston is a child of the air-conditioning that made a forbidding climate more habitable. Factors associated with the distribution of population, such as its size and the density, in turn determine which areas make demands—for highways, educational facilities, medical facilities, etc.—and which demands are met by the polity.

The social environment is determined by the ethnic, racial, and religious minorities and majorities that live in the state. Some states have relatively homogeneous populations; others, such as Texas, have highly diverse ones. The responses politicians make to the minority groups in their diverse constituencies vary. In some states they accede to the demands; in others they temper the demands by inviting minority interests into "the Establishment"; in still others vested interests refuse even to listen. As we shall see, Texas in this decade faces many such demands and the manner of response is in doubt.

The economic environment consists not only of the amount and type of wealth in a state (as measured by variety of industries, levels of banking activity, total income, etc.) but by how that wealth is distributed. Texas has long had a reputation as a wealthy state, but that reputation was built upon the notion of a state blessed with several rich industrial complexes— the oil, cattle, and cotton of the past matched by the burgeoning service, space, and banking industries of the present. But, as we will see in Chapter 4, Texas wealth is concentrated. In 1959, for example, although the median annual family income of Texans was $4884, only 12 percent of families earned more than $10,000 per year. The unequal distribution of wealth has been one of the major sources of demands from the underprivileged (particularly in cities) for state and federal responses to their plight.

The constitutional environment consists of the written and unwritten rules of a political system for representing demands and for resolving the conflicts between them. These rules specify what participants control the conversions of inputs into outputs. In general there are three basic types of such rules in state political systems. First, the rules specify a fragmentation of governing authority among various agencies of the polity: a separation of power among executive, legislative, administrative, and judicial officials. Second, constitutional rules frequently place restrictions on the authorities; in Texas, for example, a Governor cannot promulgate laws but can only accede to or veto those presented by the legislature. Third, constitutional rules endeavor to provide for representation of popular demands by having governing officials elected by qualified voters. Frequently, however, such elections provide only a symbol, or myth, of control by the populace over governing processes; instead of reflecting policies in accordance with sometimes vaguely expressed popular wishes, they reflect the bargained compromises of officials representing vested interests. The character of politics in many states, and certainly Texas, is shaped markedly by these constitutional patterns of fragmentation, restriction, and representation (a point we shall explore in detail in Chapters 4 and 5).

Finally, a state political system is embedded in a cultural environment. Culture is the habitual way in which people think of and react to one another —patterns of thought and behavior that have existed for many generations. A political culture is the basic attitude of citizens toward what government is, how it should act, and how well it performs. For example, what do citizens *know* of politics? Do they follow political affairs regularly? Do they know something of major issues and decisions of government? Do they understand the role of a Governor or of their legislator? Moreover, what do they *believe* about how government should act? Do they think politicians should take bribes? Do they believe in rights of free speech for all? Do they favor permitting every man a vote? Finally, how do they *evaluate* the performance of government? Do they take pride in their state? Do they trust state leaders or are they suspicious? Do they agree that their political roles are important to officials or do they feel officials simply don't care about average citizens?[8]

Taken together, knowledge, beliefs, and evaluations of citizens affect the style of a state's politics. For instance, the political culture is reflected in the types of people who enter politics—sons of prestigious families such as the Roosevelts, Rockefellers, or Harrimans in New York; downhome types such as the Longs or Jimmy Davis in Louisiana; rags-to-riches types such as Lyndon Johnson and John Connally in Texas. We see political culture manifested in the access to and control of policy-making by various minorities; contrast the Irish and Italian influence in Massachusetts with the relative absence of effective presence of Mexican-Americans in Texas. We see political culture at work in partisan alignments—the influence

---

[8]Gabriel Almond, "Comparative Political Systems," *The Journal of Politics*, 18 (1956), 391–409.

of party bossess in Illinois, the merchandised politics of California, or the constant bickering between liberal and conservative Democrats in Texas.

In discussing political culture in this fashion we do not mean to imply that a state is limited to only one orientation. Indeed, the larger the physical size of a state, the greater its social and economic diversity, and the more fragmented, restricted, and symbolic its constitutional structure, the more we expect a heterogeneous political culture. In such a state it would be impossible to say which of the various environments most shapes the character of politics, and it is our contention that Texas is such a state.[9] The style of Texas politics reflects the many differing political subcultures of the far West Texas, the Gulf Coast Texas, the Rio Grande Valley Texas, the Establishment Texas, the Black Texas, the Metro Texas, etc. It seems unlikely that perhaps Texas politics in the 1970s will reform the many cultures into one.

# THE PROCESSES OF STATE POLITICAL SYSTEMS

We have described a political system as a set of responses role participants make to environmental stresses; the stresses arise as inputs, affect policy-making, and are converted to outputs. Let us examine these input, output, and conversion processes for regulating conflict.

### THE INPUT PROCESS

There are two general types of inputs that flow from the environment to the polity: demands and supports. A *demand* is "an expression of opinion that an authoritative allocation with regard to a particular subject matter should or should not be made by those responsible for doing so."[10] The sources of demands are the endless variety of things people want to improve their lives. When expressed to political authorities, wants became demands

---

[9]There is an impressive body of research, however, that suggests, taking the states collectively, that the socioeconomic environments of states have a greater influence than constitutional features on shaping policy outputs as measured by the public expenditures of the states. See, for example, Richard I. Hofferbert, "The Relation Between Public Policy and Some Structural and Environmental Variables in the American States," *American Political Science Review*, LX, No. 1 (March 1966), 73-82; Ira Sharkansky, "Government Expenditures and Public Services in the American States," *American Political Science Review*, LXI, No. 4 (December 1967), 1066-77; John Crittenden, "Dimensions of Modernization in the American States," *American Political Science Review*, LXI, No. 4 (December 1967), 989-1001; and Thomas R. Dye, *Politics, Economics and the Public* (Chicago: Rand McNally & Company, 1966).

[10]Easton, *A Systems Analysis*, p. 39.

and thus the substance of political inputs. It is in this sense that the input process represents social wants for governmental consideration.

Many demands deal with very specific items and call for tangible policy responses. In Texas, for example, public school teachers (acting through their lobby, the Texas State Teachers Association) periodically demand increases in pay; sometimes the Texas Legislature responds with specific appropriations, often it does not. Other demands, however, may be general, diffuse, and vague: those to protect Texas consumers against high prices, hidden taxes, exorbitant interest rates, or excessive automobile insurance rates frequently carry no specific proposals for how to achieve these goals. Since every Texas politician wants to "protect the consumer," political oratory always agrees with the demands; official actions, however, seldom measure up to these symbolic utterances.

But, whether the demands be specific or general, there is always political conflict between interests expressing different wants. If the number and intensity of the conflicts are great, there may be a severe strain on the capacity of the governing officials to respond. On the other hand, if few demands are made (that is, if citizens feel they can better achieve their aims by turning elsewhere than to politics), the political system's function of setting goals and resolving conflict declines. The trick of politicians, in Texas and other states, is to moderate environmental stresses within tolerable limits, avoiding either explosive or moribund conditions.

Supports are the other general category of political inputs. *Supports* refer to the allegiances, loyalties, and obligations members of society are willing to have to the polity and its policies. Citizens commit their support for a variety of reasons: for fear force will be used if they disobey laws, because they believe it is in their individual economic, social, religious, or other interest to do so, or perhaps out of habit and indifference. Whatever the source of support, a political system cannot perform its critical conflict-regulating function without this essential input.

We have already touched upon the major types of support for the polity in our discussion of political culture and resources—the expectations of people about government constitute one form of such support. These expectations include the ideas citizens have "regarding what the government ought to do and the way its citizens ought to, or probably will, behave."[11] In Texas, for instance, there is no general loss of confidence in government when Texas public officials frequently advance their economic interests during their incumbencies. Although stealing from the state treasury is hardly condoned, it seems expected that Texas politicians will use their influence to build a source of wealth from various "outside" interests—con-

---

[11]Mitchell, *The American Polity*, p. 15.

struction, motels, real estate, or legal practices. Another form of support is the resources which are material—money, time, land, labor, and natural resources—and nonmaterial—prestige, reputation, rights, freedom. We observed earlier that in material resources Texas is fortunate; it has one of the largest untapped tax bases of any state. But, as we shall see, the unequal distribution of nonmaterial resources has made it difficult for the state to marshall its considerable material wealth to respond to increasing demands.

State political systems have a number of channels routing inputs from their respective environments to the polities. In Texas the principal conduits for supports are elections, political parties, the mass media, and the family and schools when they perform political socialization functions (see Chapter 3). Political demands in Texas tend to be channeled primarily through pressure groups and public officials (see Chapters 4 and 5).

## THE OUTPUT PROCESS

Since the political system is always open to its environment, receiving a steady flow of inputs, it constantly adjusts to its demands and supports. These adjustments are its outputs, the policy decisions aimed at resolving disputes in the social system over goals. In speaking of policy decisions it should be borne in mind that indecision (the refusal of governing officials to act or to accede to a demand) is also an output. For many years in Texas there have been demands from liberal elements—organized labor, intellectuals, and ethnic minorities—for the establishment of a graduated individual income tax as a means of financing improvements in schools, alleviating poverty, and establishing low cost housing. But the Texas political system has not responded positively to these demands; rather it has made policy by never adopting an income tax and repeatedly adopting sales taxes.

The fact that polities meet some demands with decisions, others with no decisions, suggests the two major types of outputs—*benefits* and *deprivations*. In large measure politics involves the continuous allocation and reallocation of benefits and deprivations, the authoritative distribution of rewards and costs among the members of society. Each policy output influences the types of future demands and supports for the polity; deprivations create new demands while benefits generate support. For example, a tax on corporations to finance improvements in education wins the support of educators but is most assuredly followed by demands from corporate leaders for its removal or redirection. Thus policy outputs, through feedback into the environment, result in policy *outcomes* permitting the polity to both adapt and to modify that environment.

The outputs of American states cover a range of matters touching the daily lives of citizens. States, sometimes alone but increasingly with federal aid, assume a major burden of the cost of public education, highway construction and maintenance, development of natural resources, health and hospitals, welfare programs, and housing and urban renewal efforts. The states play an important role in the economy by regulating businesses, unions, and the professions, establishing minimum wage standards and employment-practice laws, and through myriad other activities. And, it is the states that feel—along with cities, counties, and the federal government—major stresses generated by such phenomena as technological change, automation, air and water pollution, and population growth, but they differ in the variety and quality of policy outputs. Texas has been among the most active states in highway construction, industrial development, and construction of higher educational facilities but has responded more slowly to problems of welfare, public health, urban renewal, and air and water pollution.

As in the input process, there are channels transmitting policy outputs back to the environment. The administrative arm of state governments is a principal one; it includes the various agencies charged with law enforcement—police, tax collectors, health inspectors, licensing agencies, and others. Legislators, judges, reporters, and even teachers also serve as channels. Moreover, some of these role participants make policy as well as transmit and enforce decisions: this is the conversion process to which we now turn.

## THE CONVERSION PROCESS

As a regulative system, politics converts stress-producing demands into allocations of benefits and deprivations. This conversion process is central to the character of state systems. It is not a strictly organized, minutely planned, or continuous process; there is rarely a one-to-one relationship between demand inputs and emergent policy outputs. Nor do we often find centralized coordination and control of the means to balance conflicting demands. Instead, we have "a series of relatively autonomous processes occasionally linked on the floor of the legislature, in the chief executive's office, and by the fact that political events tend to be concentrated in the capitol and city hall."[12]

Following the general pattern, the conversion process in Texas consists of the continuous interplay of relatively autonomous policy-making coalitions, composed of diverse specialized interests, that bargain among themselves for control of small segments of state activity—the oil, railroad,

---

[12]Herbert Jacob and Michael Lipsky, "Outputs, Structure, and Power: An Assessment of Changes in the Study of State and Local Politics," *Journal of Politics*, 30, No. 2 (May 1968), 518.

or other industries; agriculture; welfare programs; education; construction; etc. Clusters of lobbyists, legislators, and administrators adjust their differences in compromises that allocate rewards to some and costs to others. Rarely do their policies differ sharply from what has always been, but incremental changes occur as these coalitions of interests adjust to new demands from the environment. More often than not (as we shall see in Chapter 6), the focus of conversion is in the biennial or annual effort to prepare a budget for determining and financing the various programs and agencies of Texas government.

Generally the conversion processes in our federal and state political systems are much alike. Because of the fragmentation and restriction discussed earlier, a large number of governing agencies—usually separated from one another in jurisdiction—jockey for control of policy-making. At the county and city levels of the American polity fragmentation is as common as on the state level. In the counties elected officials, such as clerks and treasurers, are involved in conversion as well as the nominal policy-makers, such as county commissioners. City charters frequently divide policy authority between elected councils and appointed city managers.

There are at least four phases of the conversion process. First, there is the initiation of policy proposals to meet specific demands, a responsibility assumed in Texas by legislators and, occasionally, the Governor, usually in consultation with specialized pressure groups. The second phase is the bargaining that results in the modification of initiated proposals in an attempt to satisfy contending groups; this phase usually results in formal acceptance or rejection of demands and is concentrated in the activities of legislative committees. The third phase is the application of policy decisions, dominated by bureaucratic agencies of state government which enforce laws. Because of the discretion given state officials in enforcement, however, it is not unusual to see policies altered in subtle ways. Finally, there is feedback to policy outputs: new demands or refusals to obey laws (thus calling on the judicial subsystem to adjudicate legal disputes).

Each of these conversion stages attracts the attention of differing interests seeking control of the political system. Those interested in proposal initiation focus attention on the activities of lobbyists, legislators, administrative agencies, and the Governor; interests concerned with blocking or modifying policies bargain through legislative committees; groups wanting to avoid compliance work through the state agencies; and those unwilling to accept threatening legislation make new demands or fight disagreeable laws through the courts. Given the fragmentation, differentiation, and discontinuity of the conversion process, the obvious question is: "Who controls policy-making in Texas?" To suggest how we might respond to that question in the chapters that follow, let us turn to the variations on the democratic theme in state political systems.

# THE SEARCH FOR A DEMOCRATIC POLITICAL SYSTEM IN TEXAS

Article IV, Section 4, of the Constitution of the United States states that, "The United States shall guarantee to every State in this Union a republican form of government. . . ." It is not clear what is meant by "republican form of government," but it refers to the type of control exerted over a political system by members of society.[13] Generally the republican form is synonymous with representative democracy—that is, a government in which the governed select rulers authorized to make binding policies and to be held responsible for them. Students of American politics, federal and state, have discerned three general patterns of representative democracy.[14] And although we cannot definitively answer the question of who controls policymaking in Texas, we can describe these three patterns of control and suggest, from time to time, how specific aspects of the Texas polity compare.

The first pattern we designate *participatory* democracy. Members of society select and control representatives in accordance with several conditions: (1) rulers are chosen through popular elections in which each citizen has one vote, and the rule of the majority prevails; (2) popular consultation among citizens and with representatives is assured through guarantees of unfettered communication (free speech and press), rights to organize and express demands (free assembly), and equality of education opportunities to permit access to vital information; (3) political leaders accept responsibilities to govern according to rules that include continuing review of their actions and toleration of citizens' rights, especially that to express differing points of view; (4) political equality is assured not only through equal voting rights and educational opportunities but through protections of the law—no action shall be taken unfairly against one group nor special privileges assured others; and (5) all other essential political liberties are assured—freedom of conscience, movement, access to officials, etc. Essentially, this pattern of representative government depends on the full and continuous participation of highly motivated, informed, and rational citizens with access to policymaking centers.[15] As we shall see, the pattern rarely prevails in Texas politics (indeed, it may not be even a goal of many interests); it is at best only approximated in the organization of supports for the Texas polity (see Chapter 3).

---

[13]See Edward S. Corwin, *The Constitution and What it Means Today* (12th ed.), (Princeton: Princeton University Press, 1958).

[14]Mitchell, *The American Polity*, pp. 75-94.

[15]The elements of democratic government are covered in Henry B. Mayo, *An Introduction to Democratic Theory* (New York: Oxford University Press, Inc., 1960).

A second pattern we label *pluralist* democracy. It too contains popular elections of officials, popular consultation, responsive political leadership, and guarantees of political equality and liberty. But, it differs from participatory democracy in a major essential. In the pluralist pattern control over elected officials (that is, access to policy-making or conversion processes) comes not from the citizenry's direct and continuous contact with officials but from their membership in special interest groups acting through group leaders. In other words, the pluralist model differentiates between the roles of citizens (who, with the exception of elections, are largely passive), the roles of group leaders (who speak for their membership), and the roles of officials (who hear the demands of group leaders and modify them in the bargaining phase of conversion).[16] In Chapter 4 we observe that the expression of demands in the Texas polity conforms only partially to this pluralist pattern.

Our third pattern is *elitist* democracy, although "democracy" may well be a misnomer to designate elitist rule. As we suggested, democracy implies that policy-makers are responsive and responsible to the mass citizenry, and both the participatory and pluralist patterns reflect this. Under elitist conditions, however, the ruling oligarchy (composed of elected officials, powerful economic interests, and prestigious opinion leaders) govern in the interests of the "Establishment"—i.e., themselves. As they convert demands into benefits, oligarchs retain the major rewards and distribute the costs (in the form of high sales taxes or inadequate housing, health, and public facilities) to the citizenry, thus assuring the continued control of the elite. If faced with too embarrassing a challenge from aggrieved elements, elitists restrict the opposition's access to the news media, crack down on freedom of expression, and deny essential budgetary funds, patronage, and other benefits.[17] In some respects (but not all) the conversion process in Texas has fit such a pattern of elitist democracy.

Much of what we have said of our approach to Texas politics appears in Figure 1-1. In sum, our interest centers on the Texas political system, those patterned interactions relevant to the regulation of conflicting social demands in the state. We discuss how various role participants relate to one another, giving rise to inputs from the peculiar Texas environment (Chapter 2) in the form of supports from the political culture (Chapter 3) and demands from social groups (Chapter 4). We examine how the bargains and compromises forged in Texas political institutions convert inputs to policy

---

[16]A standard introduction to the pluralist pattern is David B. Truman, *The Governmental Process* (New York: Alfred A. Knopf, Inc., 1958).

[17]See C. Wright Mills, *The Power Elite* (New York: Oxford University Press, Inc., 1956).

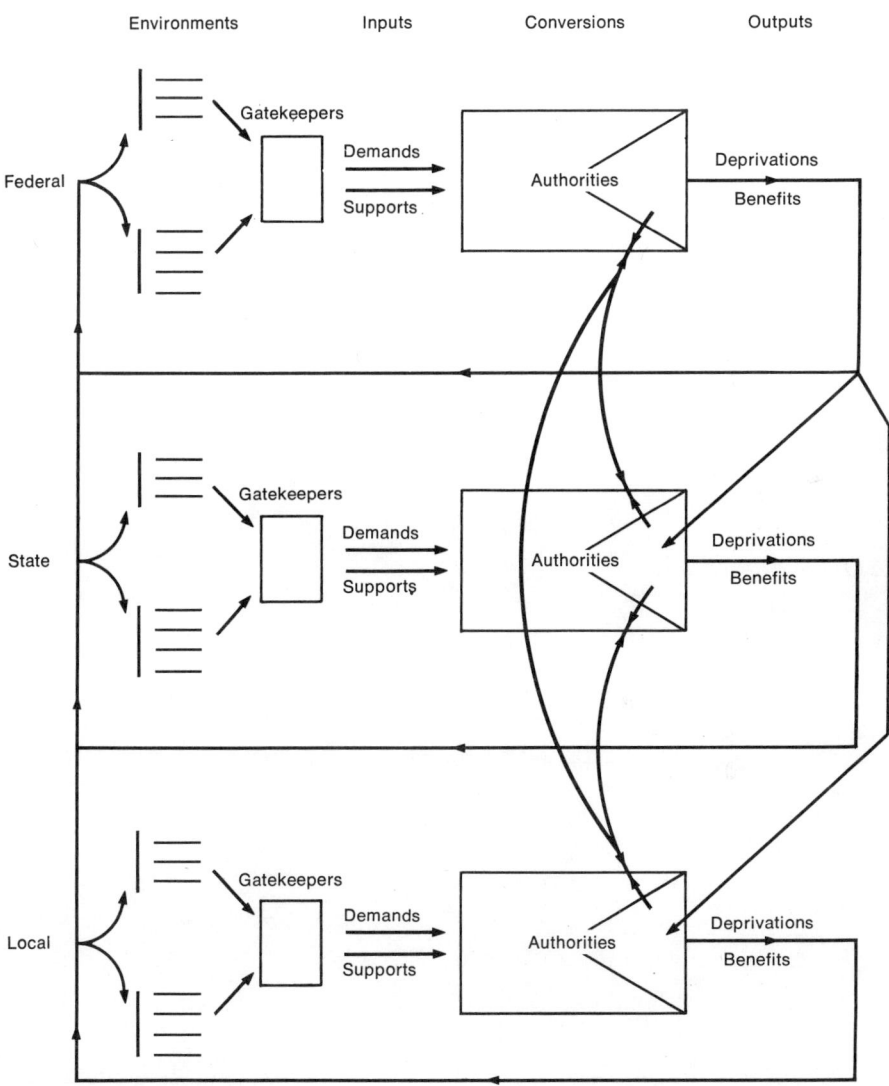

FIGURE 1-1. The multi-level political system

outputs (Chapters 5 and 6). Finally, we assess the state of these interactions as the Texas political system moves toward democracy in the 1970s (Chapter 7).

# 2
# The Environment of Texas Politics

The transactions between a political system and its environment leave their mark upon both. The inputs of state political systems vary widely depending upon differing social, economic, constitutional, and cultural confines. The dirt farmer, for example, has an interest different from the automobile mechanic or the rancher. Or, the supports and demands of Catholics regarding the political system are likely to contrast sharply with those of Protestants, especially fundamentalists. Thus, to understand the fascinating variety of the Texas political system, we must examine its ethnic character, economic background, legitimate institutions, and political culture. In this chapter we consider the social, economic, and constitutional environment of Texas politics and introduce major themes to be developed in later discussions of political demands; then, in Chapter 3 we describe the relevance of the cultural context of supports for the Texas polity.

## THE SOCIOECONOMIC ENVIRONMENT OF TEXAS POLITICS

When people migrate they take with them their social and intellectual traditions and their knowledge of how to gain a living. Although a few "start fresh," most simply transfer their way of life to new locations. Agricultural skills and living patterns, for instance, are likely to be repeated by the new immigrant. Those who ranched will continue to ranch; those who farmed will continue to farm. People from cotton country will continue to grow cotton. Old ways are repeated either until they succeed or until failure teaches migrants to do something else. Thus, the traditions, habits, and economic ways of the migrant are important to understanding both the politics of the past and the present.

## THE ETHNIC MINORITIES OF TEXAS

People outside Texas typically view the "Texan" as a native-born Anglo with a pride born of deep ancestral roots in Texas soil. The image is only partially correct. 1970 estimates of the population place the total at 11 million but indicate that slightly less than 80 percent of Texans are white. However, the image ignores the diversity of the Texas population. To be white is not necessarily to be Anglo; indeed in 1960, 15 percent of the state's white population had Spanish surnames indicating Mexican-American stock. To be a white Texan is not necessarily to be native-born Texan; in 1960, for example, more than a million Texans were first- or second-generation foreign stock: 61 percent were Mexican, 10 percent German, 4 percent United Kingdom, 3 percent Czechoslovakian, 3 percent Canadian, and 3 percent Italian. Again, the image ignores the increasingly sizable migrations of persons to Texas from all regions of the United States. More than 1 percent of Texans in 1960 had entered from out of the state since 1950, and in the 1970's the proportion may be higher; and in 1960, 21 percent of Texans were listed as having been born in another state while 3 percent were born outside of the United States or had unknown birthplaces. Finally, the image overlooks that 12 percent of Texans are black, a fact with ever-widening implications for the state's politics.[1]

Figure 2-1 illustrates the diversity of the Texas population. It shows the areas of the state with above average concentrations of Mexican-Americans, blacks, first- or second-generation immigrants, or out-of-state immigrants. Note that the concentrations are not always overlapping. The Mexican-Americans and minorities of foreign parentage are concentrated in South and Southwest Texas; blacks populate East Texas in heavy proportions; and migration was heaviest into the counties of West Texas between 1950 and 1960. To get a better picture of the heterogeneity of the Texas population, let us look at the three major ethnic groupings—the Mexican-Americans, the blacks, and the Germans.

---

[1] *A Decade of Population Change in Texas* (College Station, Texas: Texas A & M University, Agricultural Experiment Station, B-1000, September 1963), pp. 22-27.

The Environment of Texas Politics  21

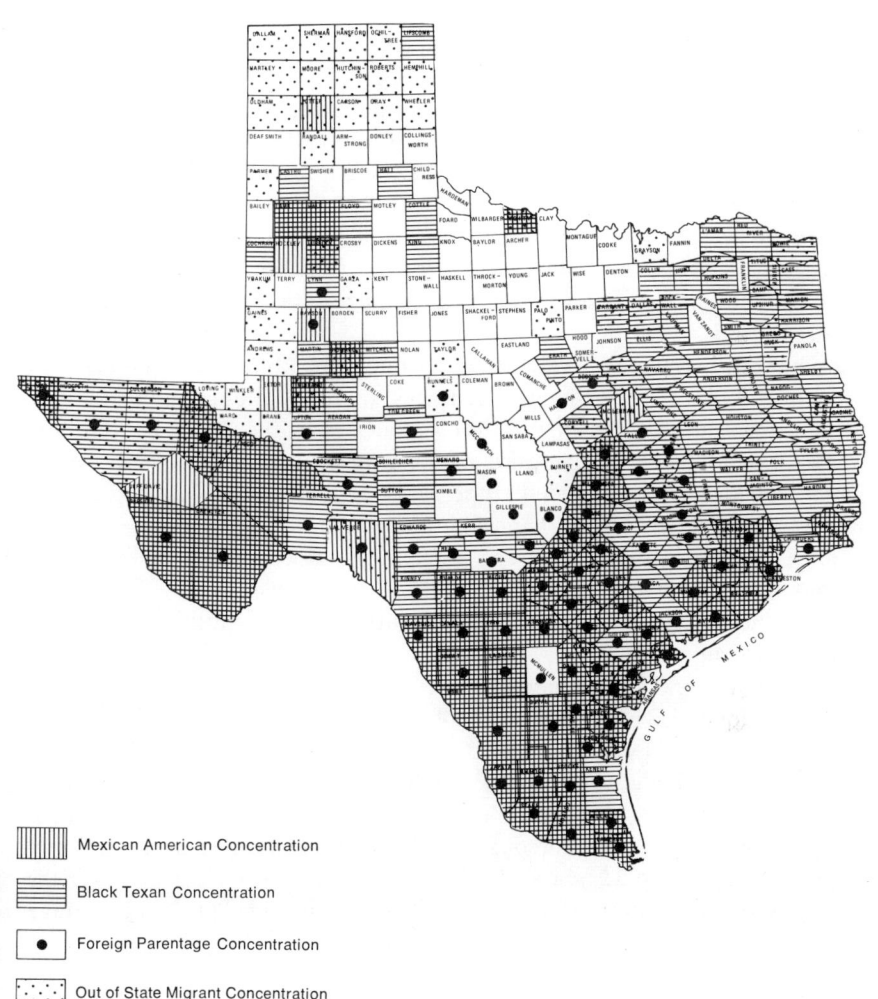

FIGURE 2-1. The distribution of minorities by Texas Counties, 1960

## The Mexican-Americans

The Spaniards set foot in Texas in 1528 when Cabeza de Vaca crossed part of southern Texas. After other explorers ventured into the area, missions were established in 1690 and the Spanish influence became permanent. Most of the missions were first established in the southern part of the region with expansion of settlements starting in earnest around 1745. San Antonio was the hub of the settlements with the office of the governor located there. Immigration and colonization continued unabated, past the Texas War of Independence and the Mexican War, until today. In 1960, Texas reported that nearly 15 percent of its population had Spanish surnames.[2] Twenty-two counties had more than 10,000 people with Spanish surnames; in the populations of five counties more than 75 percent had Spanish surnames—Jim Hogg, Webb, Maverick, Starr, and Kenedy.[3] Between 50 and 74.9 percent of the population had Spanish surnames in the counties of Jeff Davis, Zavala, Frio, Dimmit, LaSalle, Duval, Jim Wells, Brooks, Hidalgo, Willacy, Cameron, and Zapata. Twelve counties had populations of which between 50 and 74.9 percent had Spanish surnames; these counties are along the Rio Grande, eleven of them in the tier of counties in the lower Rio Grande Valley extending about one-third of the way up the river. Twenty Texas counties had between 35 and 49.9 percent and ten counties had between 25 and 34.9 percent Spanish surnames in the population.

The counties having a large percentage of people with Spanish surnames are those demographers have labeled "underdeveloped." Their populations characteristically have little education, large families, and a high unemployment rate.

*Education.* The median amount of schooling of the people in the counties along the lower one-third of the Rio Grande is less than six to nine years.[4] Of those over 25 years old with Spanish surnames, 23 percent report no formal education. These conditions have been changing in recent years, but the change has been relatively insignificant. During the 1950-1960 period, the proportion of persons over 25 years old with Spanish surnames who completed 9 to 12 years of school had increased 62 percent over the previous decade.[5] On the other hand, between 1950 and 1960 the percentage

---

[2]U.S. Bureau of Census, *U.S. Census of Population: 1960, Subject Reports, Persons of Spanish Surnames* Final Report, PC (2) 1-B (Washington, D.C.: Government Printing Office, 1962). The actual count was 1,417,811 people with Spanish surnames.

[3]Stanley A. Arbingast, Lorrin G. Kennamer, and Michael E. Bonine, *Atlas of Texas* (Austin: Bureau of Business Research, The University of Texas, 1967), p. 29.

[4]*Ibid.*, p. 49.

[5]Harley L. Browning and S. Dale McLemore, *A Statistical Profile of the Spanish Surname Population of Texas* (Austin: Bureau of Business Research, The University of Texas, 1964), p. 29.

reporting no schooling had dropped only 4.9 percent, from 27.8 to 22.9, and the percentage with 1 to 8 years of schooling had dropped only 3.4 percent, from 60.2 to 56.8.[6]

*Family.* Because of tradition and religion, the family unit of the Mexican-American is considerably larger than that of other groups. Nearly 25 percent of the families with Spanish surnames have seven or more people, compared with 3.7 percent of white families and 15.1 percent of nonwhite families. The large family unit possibly occurs for two reasons: first, the group has the highest percentage of single females in the 20-24 age group, and many of them live at home; second, once married, the fertility rate of the Spanish surname group is higher than the white or nonwhite. Nearly 27 percent report four or more children while only 8 percent of whites and 17.2 percent of nonwhites report this number.[7]

*Employment.* A lack of formal education forces Mexican-Americans to take menial and poorly paying jobs. With no industrial skills, they tended for years to be exclusively agricultural workers, following the harvest during the late summer and fall. Lack of education plus seasonal agricultural employment also destines them to a high unemployment rate. In 1964, Webb, Hidalgo, and Cameron, all border counties with large Mexican-American populations, reported 12.1, 9.6, and 8.4 percent unemployment, respectively.[8] Partly because of the high unemployment rate in these rural counties, many Mexican-Americans are emigrating to the industrialized cities such as Houston. Harris County (Houston) had a 91 percent increase in Spanish surnames from 1950 to 1960. El Paso, Nueces (Corpus Christi), and Bexar (San Antonio) counties reported close to a 50 percent increase in Spanish surnames.

This movement to the city modifies the political style of the Mexican-American citizen. Perhaps because of his small amount of formal education—lacking advantages of literacy, job opportunities, and political knowledge associated with completed schooling—he has been inclined to take his political cues from political bosses promising favors. The inclination produces, and is reinforced by, the *patron* style in which small-time political bosses control blocs of Mexican-American votes with promises of patronage jobs, financial assistance, legal advice, and not-too-subtle intimidation. The *patron* style may explain the differences between counties such as Hidalgo and Cameron which have almost identical economic interests but differ widely in their voting patterns. It generates a politics dominated by individuals rather than by interests. Some of the "Valley" counties (predominantly Mexican-American in population) have "bloc voting" constit-

---

[6]*Ibid.*, p. 30.
[7]*Ibid.*, pp. 25-27.
[8]*Ibid.*, p. 14.

uencies where a great percentage of the vote is given to one man or candidate. The Duke of Duval (county) is still remembered in Texas politics as one such infamous boss.

Voting studies remark that the unschooled and poor, Protestant or Catholic, manifest a low degree of political participation. It is one of the curious facts of a democracy that the poor have fewer demands and provide more supports that those who are better off. This has been the case with the Mexican-American in Texas for many years. His political behavior revolves around the *patron* who orders his universe for him and articulates his demands. This pattern extends beyond the rural areas into cities such as San Antonio where the paternalism of the local Mexican-American elite "makes mobilization of lower-income groups difficult."[9]

The *patron* function may be undergoing changes in the 1970s. Other leaders are trying to order the universe of the Mexican-American people by creating such organizations as the League of United Latin American Citizens, or LULAC (the oldest), PASO (the Political Association of Spanish-Speaking Organizations), and more recently, RAZA, a militant "brown power" group ("La Raza Unida") which is attempting to be a more radical political force than the others. These organizations and their leaders act as gatekeepers instead of the gatekeeper's gatekeeper. The wants of Mexican-Americans may be translated directly into demands instead of being relayed to local bosses who might or might not communicate them to the authorities. Such organizations articulate demands not just to the authorities but to private groups as well, such as Coors Brewing Company or California grape growers. At El Paso in August 1969, the Mexican-American student group, Chicanos, asked the National Students' Association to support a boycott of California table grapes by colleges and universities. They also asked for courses in Mexican-American history in the colleges and universities in the Southwest.

There are also other indications of expanded political activity from Mexican-Americans. More Mexican-Americans are seeking and winning public office, as illustrated by Congressman Henry B. Gonzalez's long tenure and the election of Mexican-Americans to control the government of Crystal City in the early 1960s. With the removal of the poll tax as a precondition for voting, Mexican-American groups have had some success in increasing the proportions of the ethnic minority registered to vote, particularly in metropolitan areas such as Houston and San Antonio.

---

[9]James R. Soukup, Clifton McCleskey, and Harry Holloway, *Party and Factional Division in Texas* (Austin: The University of Texas Press, 1964), p. 53.

## The Black Texans

Most of the Anglos who settled in the north and east of Texas were southern. In 1821, Moses Austin received permission to establish a colony of three hundred families. In 1822, Jared E. Groce arrived from Georgia with fifty wagons and ninety slaves.[10] Slaves and cotton were a way of life for the early settlers, and by 1860 there were 182,566 slaves in Texas and 21,878 slaveowners.[11] After the Civil War the number of blacks coming into Texas declined but their total number has steadily increased. In 1960, there were 1,187,125 Negroes in Texas—12 percent of the total population. Black Texans still live mainly in the area they first settled when tied to the agricultural way of life of North, Central, and East Texas. The counties in which blacks comprised more than 15 percent of the total population in 1960 are all located east of Travis County (Austin),[12] and nine of them contained 60 percent of the state's black population. In 1960 Harris County (Houston) had the largest black population (291,851), and Dallas County had the second largest (137, 954). Nine other counties of East Texas had between 35 and 55 percent of their population made up of black Texans.[13]

For the last 40 years the counties both of the Valley and of East Texas have had difficulty maintaining their population growth; this difficulty has occurred in all areas of the country which were settled early and whose farms were therefore small and geared to the draft animal. The exodus from these counties began with the introduction of the tractor and intensified farming in the 1930s. Blacks in particular have left rural areas for urban counties, seeking employment and a better life. As they move, they change occupations. Thus, "in 1930 roughly 43 percent of the gainfully employed Negroes were engaged in agriculture . . ."[14] but in 1960 only about seven percent were so employed. The majority hold the following kinds of jobs: craftsman and operative (21.6 percent), private household worker (21.4 percent), service worker (22.8 percent), and nonfarm laborer (16 percent).[15]

The median income of the black, regardless of where he lives, as approximately one-half that of his white counterpart.[16] Whereas the urban

---

[10]Rupert Norval Richardson, *Texas, The Lone Star State* (2nd ed.), (Englewood Cliffs, N. J.: Prentice-Hall, Inc., 1958), p. 48.
[11]*Ibid.*, pp. 162–63.
[12]*A Decade of Population Change in Texas*, p. 23.
[13]Arbingast, Kennamer, and Bonine, *Atlas of Texas*, p. 28.
[14]James Reese, "Labor in Texas," *The Handbook of Texas*, Vol. III (Austin: The Texas State Historical Association, 1970).
[15]*The Nonwhite Population of Texas* (College Station, Texas: Texas A. & M. University, Agriculture Experiment Station, 1966), p. 13. Negroes make up all but 1.5 percent of the nonwhite population of Texas; hence, the terms Negro and nonwhite are used synonymously.
[16]*Ibid.*, p. 13.

white person's median income is $5693, the urban black's is $2915. The rural black fares even worse: the median income of the nonwhite employed male over 14 years is only 46 percent of the white median income. The median income for a rural white Texas family is $3201 but $1430 for a black one.[17] In Chapter 4 we will explore the impact upon political demands of these differentials in the quality of life between black and white, urban and rural dweller.

## The German-Texans

Starting in 1843, the Association for the Protection of German Immigrants in Texas stimulated the influx of Germans to Texas. Prince Carl of Solms-Braunfels was the sponsor of the association. From settlements in New Braunfels and Fredericksburg the group spread out through the Hill Country and Edwards Plateau. The area is primarily agricultural and rural with a smattering of cities and towns. Depending upon the classification scheme used, there are from 10 to 16 German counties in Texas. At a minimum the following counties could be so classified: Austin, Comal, De Witt, Fayette, Gillespie, Guadalupe, Kendall, Lee, Medina, and Washington. In addition, Colorado, Golaid, Kerr, Mason, Lavaca, and Victoria counties have sizable proportions of German-Texans. The German counties had a median annual family income in 1959 varying from $2408 to $3643 as compared with the state's median of $4884.

Coming from Europe during the middle of the nineteenth century, the Germans had little use or sympathy for slavery; even today there is a low percentage of blacks in German counties. In the Civil War they were pro-Union or were neutral; they attached themselves to the Republican Party during Reconstruction and still possess Republican sentiments. They have perpetuated much of the German attitude toward work and individual responsibility, although modern communication and mobility, as well as marriage outside of the community, have eroded the cultural patterns and atmosphere of German Texas. Indeed, the lingering support for Republican candidates is probably due more to economic interests than historical traditions.[18]

*THE CHANGING ECONOMIC
BACKGROUND OF TEXAS
POLITICS*

Dating at least as far back as Aristotle, students of politics have been fascinated with the relationship between economics and political life. Are

---

[17]*Ibid.*, p. 25.
[18]Soukup, McCleskey, and Holloway, *Party and Factional Division*, pp. 39-40.

governments operated in the interests of economic elites? Do men vote simply by their pocketbooks? Does democratic stability depend upon the existence of a widespread middle class? In keeping with the tradition, students of comparative state politics have endeavored to measure the relative impact of economic, social, and political inputs upon the policy outputs of state political systems. Their findings, although not conclusive, suggest that factors related to the states' economic development (such as urbanization, industrialization, and revenue sources) may be better indicators of the amounts states will spend on education, health and welfare, highways, taxation, or police protection than types of state party systems, levels of voting participation, or other political considerations.[19] At any rate, such research highlights the importance of the economic environment of a state polity and prompts us to consider three dimensions of the Texas economy shaping political supports and demands—urbanization, industrialization, and economic development.

## Urbanization

One of the most striking things about Texas is its increasing urbanization. This has been caused particularly by changes in agricultural technology, industrialization, and migration following industrialization.

The consequences of advances in agricultural technology are illustrated by comparing agriculture in 1930 and 1964. During this time, the tractor began to drive both black and white tenants off the land and into the cities, by reducing the necessity for human labor. The number of tenants declined from 301,660 in 1930 to 37,080 in 1964. Over the years there was a steady decline in the number of farms of less than fifty acres and an increase in the number of farms over 500 acres. The average size of the farm increased from 252 acres in 1930 to 691 acres in 1964, while the total number of farms dropped from 495,489 to 205,110. As the tractor became more common, the land necessary to pasture and support draft animals could be used instead for increased production of crops for human consumption. In 1930, there were 11,156,355 acres of pasture; five years later there were 7,786,697 acres.[20] Persons driven from the land to the cities during the thirties provided the labor for the industrialization of Texas during the following decade.

---

[19]Representative of such comparative state studies are Thomas R. Dye, *Politics, Economics, and the Public: Policy Outcomes in the American States* (Chicago: Rand McNally & Company, 1966) and Ira Sharkansky, *Spending in the American States* (Chicago: Rand McNally & Company, 1968). See, however, Charles F. Cnudde and Donald J. McCrone, "Party Competition and Welfare Policies in the American States," *American Political Science Review*, LXIII (September 1969), 858-66.

[20]U.S. Bureau of Census, *Agricultural Census, 1964* (Washington, D.C.: U.S. Government Printing Office, 1964), pp. 7, 10.

The mechanization of the farm had a second profound effect upon the economy of rural and near-rural counties. Modern machinery reduced the number of children needed to work on the land, and the size of rural families decreased as well as the number of farms. With a decreasing farm population, the total amount of consumer goods purchased declined and the small-town merchant experienced declining sales. Even if he captured all of the business in these rural areas, the amount was not sufficient to sustain him. Soon shopkeepers too left the small town for larger markets.

*Political effects.* The Farmers Union, which grew during the depression and represented the small farmer, began to be replaced by the more conservative Farm Bureau, which represented the large farmer. The small farmer remained tied to the Democratic Party while the large farmer, with large investments in land and machinery, became more conservative and more Republican.[21] The small merchant who moved to a larger city, having been threatened by failure which he did not cause and was unable to stop, became more conservative, too, and also began to move from the Democratic to the Republican Party. The vote of some urban centers in Texas became more conservative than the rural vote.

Texas' population increased during the sixties by 14.7 percent as compared to the national increase of 11.7 percent. The rate of increase in the sixties was impressive but did not match the 24 percent growth rate of the fifties. Preliminary information from the 1970 census indicated a Texas population of 10,989,123 making Texas the most populated state after California (19,696,940), New York (17,979,712), and Pennsylvania (11,663,301). Population growth in the sixties was not distributed evenly in the state. Generally, counties gaining residents were those with the state's metropolitan centers and the coastal counties. By 1970, four metropolitan areas (Houston, Dallas, Fort Worth, and San Antonio) accounted for almost 50 percent of the state's population. The coastal counties, because of their industrial and recreational potential, proved attractive; Galveston, for example, increased by 18 percent and Brazoria by 40 percent. Other areas of the state, however, either lost residents or stabilized the population growth that had started in the 1950s. Rural areas declined as urban centers attracted Texans. (The census definition of an urban area is one in which there are 2500 or more people who live in a contiguous territory or in incorporated areas; this is an arbitrary figure and does not mean that all urban residents in Texas have developed urban attitudes!) Counties in West Texas, which had experienced phenomenal population growths in the fifties tended to level off in the sixties, an indication that their growth is being affected by deficiencies in potential water supplies. Finally, as in other states, the suburbs grew

---

[21]This is shown clearly in Soukup, McCleskey, and Holloway, *Party and Factional Division*, Chap. IV.

rapidly in Texas in the sixties, sometimes at the expense of surrounding rural areas and frequently at the expense of center cities (Beaumont, for example, decreased in population by 3 percent and Amarillo by 10 percent in the decade).[22]

## Industrialization

The urbanization and industrialization of Texas occurred simultaneously; that is, as more people moved to town, manufacturing increased. "The value added by manufacture jumped from one-half billion dollars in 1939 to five billion dollars in 1959."[23] The farm population declined from 40 percent of the total population in 1940 to less than 10 percent in 1960. The petro-chemical industry has contributed to this rapid industrialization more than any single industry. Harris County has become the center of heavy industry while Dallas-Tarrant counties have become the center of light industry as well as the financial center of Texas.

Unions have grown along with industry and rural exodus to industrial areas. However, Texas membership in labor unions has not been very substantial. In 1960, there were over 400,000 union members; about 375,000 of these were in the AFL-CIO. However, estimates are that this proportion declined in the 1960s.[24] The principal growth in unions has been along the Gulf Coast around Beaumont and Houston where new heavy industries have flourished; about one-half of the state's union membership is in this area. The light industry around Dallas-Fort Worth produces fewer members: about one-third of the total state membership. The rest of the membership is scattered in the oil-field refinery industry around Borger, Odessa, and Tyler. Small industries, especially those employing less than 250 workers, have traditionally been unorganized.

In other rapidly industrialized states labor unions have generally grown and prospered, but not in Texas; perhaps because Texans have never been especially sympathetic to collective action for social and economic improvement (see Chapter 3). The political myths (always difficult to validate but important in structuring demands and supports) reflect this outlook. The jokes about Texans (perpetuated by Texans themselves) represent what they consider themselves to be or want to be and are perhaps a part of their sub-

---

[22]Preliminary estimates from the 1970 census of population appear in the following: U.S. Bureau of the Census, *1970 Census of Population: Preliminary Reports*, Texas, PC(P1)-45 (Washington, D.C.: U.S. Department of Commerce, 1970); "1970 Census," *Congressional Quarterly*, XXVIII (July 31, 1970), 1957-1963; Stanley A. Arbingast, "Some Comments on the Preliminary 1970 Census Data," *Texas Business Review*, XLIV (July 1970), 178-79.

[23]William Trout Chambers and Lorrin Kennamer, Jr., *Texans and Their Land* (Austin, Texas: Steck Company, 1963), p. 194.

[24]James Reese, "Labor in Texas."

conscious, a part of their mental world, which they act out in the political, social, and economic world. Texans have tended to caricature themselves as big, grandiose, unlimited, and unbridled. The mustang and longhorn, both products of the frontier range, are favorite symbols. Texas emerges in the folklore as a land of *individuals,* the last frontier, the place where the government allowed individual initiative and enterprise to flourish and take their rewards.

Hence, Texas has been one of the last industrial areas to admit labor's right to organize. In 1947, Texas passed a repressive labor bill, somewhat similar to parts of the later Taft-Hartley Act, as well as the right-to-work law, which forbade both closed and union shop contracts, although no penalties were provided in the statute. The legislature supplemented this law in 1951 with legislation that declared such contracts in violation of Texas anti-trust laws. In keeping with the Protestant Ethic, Texans have demanded that individual labor and its rewards be protected from too much "interference," from either the state or labor unions.

Texas political authorities, especially Congressmen, have reflected the nonunion orientations of the citizenry. In the 90th Congress, for example, Texas congressmen in the House of Representatives voted in support of American Federation of Labor and Congress of Industrial Organizations (AFL-CIO) positions in only 128 of a possible 299 cases. The Texas delegation disagreed with the AFL-CIO 53 percent of the time, expressing their fundamental sentiment, "Industrialization without Unionism."[25]

Urbanization, industrialization, and individualism combined to lend an ideological tone to Texas politics not easily matched in the other states.[26] That is, political controversies revolved about economic matters and the role of state government in advancing or thwarting economic interests. "Conservatives" advocated policies promoting commercial interests; "liberals" argued for policies restraining commercial exploitation of laboring interests and demanding that the economic advantages of employers be balanced by the rights of workers to organize. Even today businessmen migrating to Texas frequently position themselves on political issues in accordance with their perceived economic interests. Joining with the home-grown executives and junior executives who populate small business and light industry, they are likely to support conservative policies—traditionally within the conservative Democratic faction but increasingly within the Republican party. With demands normally acceptable in the political and economic climate of Texas, and with a keen ability to articulate those demands, they formulate inputs more likely to be processed by the political system than those of the poor, uneducated minorities.

---

[25]*AFL-CIO News* (XIII: 40), October 5, 1968.
[26]V. O. Key, Jr., *Southern Politics in State and Nation* (New York: Vintage Press, 1949), Chapters 12-14.

## Economic Development

Texas is not the only state where such social and economic forces as urbanization, industrialization, and unionization are redrawing the boundaries of the political system. Virtually all states, particularly in the South and Southwest, are undergoing economic development. It is worthwhile to know how Texas compares with other states in its economic "modernization" and how such changes are related to Texas political development.

To assist us in that comparison we rely upon measures of economic and political development devised by students of state politics. At the outset it is helpful to recognize that a state develops economically along several dimensions, such as urbanism and industrialization. A recent study, based upon 1960 census data, reveals three principal dimensions by which the economic development of the states may be compared.[27] The first is labeled, for sake of convenience, *Metro-Urbanism*; states developing in this respect experience marked population growth, population shifts to urban areas, large proportions of the employed in white-collar and professional occupations, sizable newspaper circulation, low fertility rates, and ethnic diversity. From our description of the ethnic and rural-urban composition of the Texas environment we would expect the state to rank fairly high in metro-urban characteristics. In fact, Texas ranks sixth among the states, following New York, California, Illinois, New Jersey, and Massachusetts.

The second dimension, *Integrative Message Exchange,* refers to characteristics that tend to facilitate communication among people—education, income, telephone availability, competition between political parties, and voting. Texas, with its relatively low educational levels, low median family income level, lack of party competition, and low voting turnouts, ranks thirty-ninth among the states on this dimension, placing it on a par with such states as Tennessee, North Carolina, Florida, and Georgia. A final dimension of economic modernization, *Migratory Pull*, relates to the proportion of citizens born out-of-state, migration into the state, and population increase. Again Texas ranks relatively high, eleventh, in the same category as Idaho, Maryland, Oregon, and Utah.

We can also rank Texas on measures of political development. As expected, for example, Texas does not rank high in measures indicating interparty competition and voting turnout, liberality of suffrage laws, turnout in gubernatorial elections, and two-party competition for governor. Along this *Competition-Turnout* dimension Texas ranks thirty-eighth, similar to Tennessee and Florida. A second political dimension, *Professionalism-Local Reliance*, permits composite rankings based upon amounts

---

[27] John Crittenden, "Dimensions of Modernization in the American States," *American Political Science Review,* LXI (December 1967), 989-1001.

of judicial and legislative salaries, expenditures on legislative services, legislative activity, and locally derived and expended funds. Texas ranks tenth, well below New York or California but at about the same level as Florida.[28] *Scope of Government* measures the size of government employment and the degree to which a state taxes and spends relative to its population size. Here Texas ranks thirty-second (along with South Carolina, New Hampshire, Illinois, and North Carolina)[29] as its relatively low taxation and expenditure rates reflect the cultural notion that in Texas government should refrain from interfering with individual "initiative" (see Chapter 3).

States may also be ranked on the basis of policy outputs as indicated by relative expenditures for certain programs. The dimension of *Welfare-Education*, for example, includes generous welfare payments, the tendency of high school pupils to remain in school until graduation, and similar characteristics. Here Texas ranks thirty-seventh, again with a pattern similar to that of Florida. On a *Highway-National Resources* dimension (including measures of rural highway mileage, expenditures for highways, fish and wildlife services, and natural resources) Texas ranks thirty-seventh, in the same general category as Florida, Georgia, Virginia, and West Virginia.[30] Finally, if states are ranked according to the speed with which they have adopted new policy ideas to solve problems, Texas is especially low-ranked. A ranking on the basis of adoption of eighty-eight programs (including merit systems for state employees, air pollution control, child labor standards, and others) lists Texas forty-second, just above South Carolina, Wyoming, Nevada, and Mississippi.[31] Certainly if conservatism means minimal changes in the status quo, this ranking underscores the conservative character of the Texas political system.

In sum, while Texas' urbanization and migration patterns suggest above average "modernization" rates in the economic environment, rates of change of political and policy development remain below those of most of the other states. A partial explanation for this is that inputs derived from a changing social and economic environment are processed by relatively stable institutions lying within the constitutional framework of the political system.

---

[28]Ira Sharkansky and Richard I. Hofferbert, "Dimensions of State Politics, Economics, and Public Policy," *American Political Science Review*, LXIII (September 1969), 867-79.

[29]Crittenden, "Dimensions of Modernization," 998.

[30]Sharkansky and Hofferbert, "Dimensions of State Politics," 876; Ira Sharkansky, "Government Expenditures and Public Services in the American States," *American Political Science Review*, LXI (December 1967), 1066-77.

[31]Jack L. Walker, "The Diffusion of Innovations Among the American States," *American Political Science Review*, LXIII (September 1969), 880-99.

# THE CONSTITUTIONAL ENVIRONMENT OF TEXAS POLITICS

Unless marked revision of the document occurs in the 1970s, by 1976 Texans will have lived with their current written constitution for a century. But, a constitution is more than simply a written contract to abide by a specified set of rules and procedures. It also embodies the traditions and habitual behaviors reflecting the political system's responses to stresses in its social, economic, and cultural milieu. In the remainder of this chapter we explore both the institutions and influences provided by the Texas Constitution.

## POLITICAL INSTITUTIONS IN TEXAS

We noted in Chapter 1 that a systems approach to the study of politics focuses upon three major features of the polity itself—the political community, the regime, and the authorities. In Texas the legitimacy and stability of each are now almost taken for granted, but this was not always the case.

## The Struggle for Political Community

States are political subsystems operating within other political systems, such as the federal government or foreign governments. Each state also has political subsystems operating within it which influence the political behavior of the people in the state. In some cases, the political institutions set the boundaries of political activity, dictate the flow of demands, determine where the demands may enter the process, and establish the sequence involved in processing demands.[32] But the political institutions, themselves, were part of the demands of the people, or the politically relevant people, at one time.

In most cases, states within the federal union do not have to be concerned with the problem of establishing their legitimacy for the exercise of authority. Legitimacy is due in part to the method in which states are established. A territory first seeks enabling legislation passed by Congress, draws up a constitution, and when accepted by joint resolution of Congress, is admitted as an equal sister state. The state does not have to establish its own legitimacy but acquires it from the federal system. Rarely will such legitimacy be questioned. It was questioned in the Civil War, and more

---

[32]David Easton, *A Systems Analysis of Political Life* (New York: John Wiley & Sons, Inc., 1965), pp. 171-219.

recently the segregationist policies of southern states have been questioned, although this hardly amounts to a wholesale challenge of the legitimacy of the state. The recent questioning of segregation has been due to the demise of racist ideology which formerly allowed, even demanded, pro-segregation policies.

Texas established its legitimacy differently; its people had first to conceive of the state as an entity and then to fight for independence. Initially they were fighting for rights as Mexicans rather than for separation. During the early part of the Texas Revolution, the state had three governments, each lasting only a short time and each trying to consolidate support and focus issues. The first government was the Permanent Council. The second, the Consultation of the Chosen Delegates of All Texas, assembled in the General Convention to draw up an organization for the Provisional Government; finally, conflict and uncertainty forced this government to give way to an Advisory Committee.[33] In December 1835, the Council called for an election of delegates to act with plenary powers. The Declaration of Independence was issued, and by this time there existed enough support to make separation possible. The delegates proposed a constitution and selected an interim government until the new constitution could be accepted, as it was in September 1836. The first crisis in legitimacy, then, was the decision to separate from an established political community and form another. A political community may be considered as "that aspect of a political system that consists of its members seen as a group of persons bound together by a political division of labor."[34] Texans left one group bound by a political division of labor and created a new one.

## The Political Regime

The second crisis involved the establishment of the *regime*—the "values (goals and principles), norms, and structure of authority."[35] System values are not always immediately clear or accepted at the start of a revolution but emerge as the revolution progresses. By the time independence had been secured in Texas, the values and norms had emerged, which simplified the task of structuring the authority. The first constitution was a product of these values and norms, first seen as inputs or demands which the old system was unable to process. Thus, constitutions become the embodiment of the basic values of the political community.

If constitutions are, as Aristotle said, a way of life, what is the significance of the numerous revisions of the Texas Constitution?

---

[33]Richardson, *Texas*, pp. 88-91.
[34]Easton, *A Systems Analysis*, p. 177.
[35]*Ibid.*, p. 193.

They have rarely reflected any basic change in the values: a successful drive for revision reflects the same values as the constitution. Major alterations in the community's value system require other measures. In most cases, revision has represented the efforts of individual or group interests to gain long-range rewards from the political system on a more permanent basis than statutes offer (see Chapter 4). Repeated constitution-making generally means that the regime values are accepted and that the struggle of individual or group interests now becomes the core of the activity.

If the Texas constitutions are compared with each other, it is apparent that the constitutions of 1836, 1845, 1861, and even 1869 did not change the regime values much. In 1845 the only basic change in the 1836 constitution was the recognition of federal supremacy after admission to the Union. In 1861, after Texas withdrew from the Union, the constitution was changed to recognize the supremacy of the Confederation, to join a new political community, and to change loyalties. After the Civil War, Texas made the identical constitutional change as in 1861: it joined a new political community (the Union) and changed loyalties. However, regime changes also took place: slavery was outlawed and the electorate changed to include blacks and exclude Confederate sympathizers until they could be cleared as loyal.

By 1872, the disenfranchised Democrats, who had traditionally controlled the state, regained control and began to work for a constitutional convention. The constitution of 1875-1876 represents a change less in regime values and goals than a fight over which interests were to be privileged. Railroad regulation, for example, became one of the important areas of conflict, along with education and public lands. Because of the resentment of the Reconstruction government of 1869, many delegates voted for detailed constraints upon future governments. The constitution was thus long and so restrictive that it required frequent future amendment and generated ever-recurring moves toward constitutional revision.[36] However, the 1876 constitution confirmed privileges for many private interests, and those who received these privileges have been reluctant to support constitutional revision for they would be required to fight the battle for privilege all over

---

[36]See Dick Smith, "Constitutional Revision in Texas, 1876-1961," *Public Affairs Comment* (Austin: Institute of Public Affairs, the University of Texas, 1969, also reprinted in Fred Gantt, Jr., Irving Dawson, and Luther Hagard, Jr., eds., *Governing Texas: Documents and Readings* (New York: Thomas Y. Crowell Co., 1966), pp. 49-55; and Dick Smith, "Constitutional Revision: Attempts to Unshackle Texas," *Public Affairs Comment* (Austin: Institute of Public Affairs, The University of Texas, 1969). For a comparison and study of continuity of regime values, see the following articles in Ernest Wallace and David Vigness, eds., *Documents of Texas History* (Austin, Texas: The Steck Company, Publishers, 1960): "The Proposed Constitution for the State of Texas, April 13, 1833," pp. 80-85; "Plan and Powers of the Provisional Government of Texas," pp. 91-93; "The Constitution of the Republic of Texas," pp. 100-105; "The Texas Constitution of 1845," pp. 149-59; and "The Constitution of 1869," pp. 213-16.

again and run the risk of losing. Aside from the risks involved, there is the cost of defending privileges. Private interests deem it safer to handle constitutional revision for such groups through citizens' committees reporting recommendations through established channels where established interest groups have mastered the processes and can manipulate them within known boundaries.[37] Even here, constitutional revision has little prospect for success. When, for example, in the 1960s an advisory commission was to be named jointly by the Governor, the Lieutenant Governor, and the Speaker of the House, Lt. Governor Preston Smith refused to name his delegates, thus destroying the legitimacy of the commission before it even started. Rule-making about rules is more serious than just making rules. Politics at the constitution-making level is serious political business, indeed.[38]

## The Political Authorities

The constitution not only embodies regime values and goals, but also imposes constraints upon both the public and the authorities. In addition, it provides structures and processes to be used in dealing with demands. These structures and processes influence behavior since they determine at which place demands can enter the system and what procedures must be followed in turning inputs into outputs. For example, demands for the resolution of private interests may enter the system through the candidate during the nomination process and campaign, or through public officials who articulate inchoate demands and make them into real demands, in the legislature, the executive or the administration, and ultimately the courts. Each of these has its own processes and norms.

What are the basic regime values of Texas, then, as embodied in the structure of authority outlined in public documents? First, Texans have

---

[37]See Duane Lockard, *The Politics of State and Local Governments* (New York: The Macmillan Company, 1963) for a development of the idea that detailed constitutions prevent both the legislature and the courts from altering privileges. Also, see Charles R. Adrian, *Government of Our Fifty States and Communities* (New York: McGraw-Hill Book Co., 1967), pp. 8–9. Lewis A. Froman, in his "Some Effects of Interest Group Strength in State Politics," *American Political Science Review*, LX (December 1966), 954-62, demonstrates a correlation between strong interest groups and the length of the constitution. J. William Davis's article in Gantt, Dawson, and Hagard, eds., *Governing Texas*, pp. 56-64, traces the attempts to get some recommendations for revision through via the Research Director of the Citizen's Advisory Committee. The struggle is, of course, politics of the first order and should be viewed in that light. What is needed is a thorough study of the politics of a constitutional convention.

[38]See T. C. Sinclair and Werner Grunbaum, *The Constitution of Texas: Personal Rights and Liberties* (Dallas: Arnold Foundation Monographs, Southern Methodist University, 1960); and J. E. Ericson, "Origins of the Texas Bill of Rights," *Southwestern Historical Quarterly*, (April 1959), 457-66.

based their system of government upon the same theory of consent which is seen in the government of the United States. This theory is drawn basically from John Locke's political philosophy. In Article I, Sections 2 and 3, the Texas Constitution states that the government is to be based on a compact. This statement has been made repeatedly, with slight variation, starting with the Texas Declaration of Independence and continuing through each constitution. Natural rights, limited government, popular sovereignty, the right to alter, abolish, or reform the government, and rights against the government are all part of the regime values inherited from Locke and expressed through succeeding constitutions. Also part of this heritage, and laid down in the Texas Bill of Rights, are freedom of religious belief, of speech and press (with the individual held responsible for abuse of this privilege), rights of the accused, and rights against *ex post facto* laws. These regime values are basically the same as those expressed in the Declaration of Independence of the United States and the Bill of Rights of the United States Constitution.

Second, Article II of the Texas Constitution states that there is to be a separation of powers into the legislative, executive, and judicial. Articles III, IV, and V relate to these branches respectively. In keeping with the Lockean faith in the legislative body, Article III is the longest and most detailed of the three. Accordingly, it has been amended more frequently than the others and now includes some 60 amendments.

The executive branch has undergone one basic change: in the Constitution of 1845, the Governor had the power to appoint state officials and the executive department was not structured except for the Governor and the Secretary of State. The Jacksonian Revolution finally changed this in Texas as it had done in many states. Jacksonians believed that any man of average intelligence could hold governmental office, that the spoils belonged to the victor, that rotation in office was good since men tended to be lax and unresponsive to public needs when left too long in office, and that the convention method of nominating within the party system was desirable. The result was to fragment power by making offices elective rather than appointive, and to use the political party system as a method of focusing and uniting this fragmented power. Students of state politics generally classify Texas as having a "weak executive" because of this fragmentation. One study ranks Texas, Mississippi, South Carolina, and North Dakota as the states with the weakest executives on the basis of their constitutionally defined budget powers, appointive powers, veto powers, and tenure.[39] It is therefore difficult to account for the strong executives that have existed in Texas unless we take into account the informal considerations that make strong

---

[39]Joseph A. Schlesinger, "The Politics of the Executive," in *Politics in the American States*, eds. Herbert Jacob and Kenneth N. Vines (Boston: Little, Brown & Co., 1965), p. 229.

gubernatorial leadership possible. The Governor's strength can be considerably enhanced, for instance, if he is head of a strong political party organization or champion of popular causes (as was James Hogg, 1891-1895, and Allan Shivers, 1949-1957, when he led the state from the Democratic to the Republican column in presidential voting), or if he enjoys such mass public support that other members running for administrative positions are compelled to give him some support also.

In 1850, Texas adopted amendments making judicial and executive positions elective. This style has become the common constitutional pattern for Texas, having been repeated with varying degrees of strictness in succeeding constitutions. The current constitution designates the executive department to consist of the Governor, the Lieutenant Governor, the Secretary of State, the Comptroller of Public Accounts, the Treasurer, the Commissioner of General Land Office, and the Attorney General. With the exception of the Secretary of State, who is appointed by the Governor, all these officials are elected. Thus, part of the regime goal has been to make executives accountable at frequent intervals, generally every two years. Recent attempts to extend the term of office for the Governor from two to four years have failed, the people having rejected such an amendment in 1969. Attempts to extend judicial terms of office have also failed. These terms are longer, however, than those of the executive: Supreme Court and Court of Criminal Appeals judges have six-year terms, while District and County judges have four-year terms. Other state and local officials have had their two-year terms increased to four.

There are three other regime values embodied in Texas constitutional law. First, it is considered unwise to have unlimited deficit financing. Hence, the Constitution specifies that the "debt created to supply deficiencies in revenue shall never exceed in the aggregate at any time two hundred thousand dollars." Second, a system of checks and balances is maintained, especially between the legislative and executive branches. This is seen in the limited appointive and removal powers of the Governor, the itemic veto of the Governor on appropriation bills, and the sharing of financial responsibility through the submission of multiple budgets. Third, ease of changing the Constitution is maintained through an amendment process which requires only two-thirds approval of both houses, publication of the amendment once a week for four weeks before the election, and acceptance by a majority of those voting.

## THE CONTEXTS OF FEDERALISM AND LOCALISM

It may seem odd to refer to the federal system as a multiple-level political system, but that is what it is. If we consider each state as a discrete political entity with its own practices, its own social environment, its own demands and supports, and its own political regime and authorities, then each is a political system in itself. Moreover, within each state there are subsystems, such as the county, city, school, and special districts, which can also be treated as political systems. Relations between and within these levels are governed by both formal and informal considerations. The formal relationship is set forth in the Constitution of the United States, which defines the power of the central government, its obligations to the states, the limitations on both the states and individuals, the obligations between states, and their obligations to the whole. The U. S. Constitution both constrains the states and grants authority to them. The state constitutions and statutes authorize the establishment of the local governmental units. The states have a unitary system rather than a federal system, since local governments do not have autonomy but exist for the administrative convenience of the state. Thus, each unit of government acts as a system within which demands can be presented and processed and supports can be developed or withheld.

It is obvious that there is a great deal of interaction between these systems. Because the Constitution of the United States forbids the states to act in certain areas, in many cases such action falls both formally and informally to the federal government. For example, one area forbidden to the states encompasses acts related to war. The states are not allowed to enter into treaties, alliances, or confederations, to have a navy or troops in time of peace without the consent of Congress, to grant letters of marque or reprisal (that is, grant commissions to a private citizen to capture and confiscate the merchant ships of any nation), or to engage in war except when actually invaded or when war is so imminent as to not admit delay. War powers are formally given to the central government, although at one time the states did perform certain peacekeeping functions along the border and in the frontier area. Since World War II, formal constraints have placed more emphasis upon denying this power to the states, since it is unlikely that any state will be invaded in an isolated sense, and, should that happen, all the states would be drawn into the conflict immediately.

Technological advancements have also changed the relationships between state systems. When the "more perfect union" was established, for example, markets were small and compact, production was geared to the available market, and people tended to be aware of the local and state governments as the systems which most directly affected them. It was in *Gibbons* v. *Ogden* (1823), thirty-four years after the establishment of the government, that the Supreme Court attempted to define the freedoms and limitations of commerce among the several states. Since that time, the commerce clause has been one of the chief objects of litigation. Territorial expansion and technological advancement also changed demands. What was previously a state function gradually became a federal function, or at least a joint enterprise.

After the Revolutionary War, America conceived of liberty and freedom in Lockean terms as a contest between man and state. Indeed, under Locke's theory all power and sovereignty belonged to the individual, and the only way for the state to get any power in the first place was to be given that power by the individuals. To increase its power, the state would have to take power from the individuals. This attitude continued unchallenged until the rise of the railroads, when it became clear that private groups could also destroy the liberty of individuals. The only reasonable alternative was to demand regulation of railroads by the state, first at the local level and ultimately at the national level. Intra- and interstate commerce commissions were created to regulate private groups. This attitude has persisted. Liberty and freedom are no longer defined in pure Lockean terms, but rather in terms of individual-group-state interaction. Thus, there has emerged a changed *ideology* which not only involves new demands but now supports governmental actions against private groups. This shift in viewpoint, however, has been more apparent on the national level than in Texas. In part, the frontier sentiment still carries over, for many Texans are prone to view liberty and freedom in terms of the two-player, zero-sum game of John Locke (witness their editorials, some of their party platforms, the absence of governmental agencies in the form of a state utilities commission, and the lack of strong labor legislation supporting the laboring group against the business group).

One of the complications of modern federalism is the almost complete interdependence of the federal and state systems. Markets are now tied together by a vast highway and rail system; producers are no longer bound to a small area, but enjoy a market which stretches from coast to coast. Individuals and groups are confused about which political system they should approach with their demands. In the face of an ideology which pleads the virtues of keeping the state system strong, appeals are made to the central government to make the local government act in a desired way.[40] It is not certain at which point political demands move from one level to another. Such movement appears to be based on many factors, such as how motivated a group is to gain a favorable solution, how cohesive the group is, what its ideologies and beliefs are, and how easily it can enlist support from related groups.

---

[40]Although viability of local government has been a generally accepted regime value in Texas, the Republican Party seems to have stressed it more than the Democratic Party has. Perhaps this is because the Republicans have been a minority in the state and thus better able to act as critics. However, it is ironic that one of the leading Republican candidates recently turned to the United States judiciary to compel Texas to reapportion according to the standards of *Reynolds* v. *Sims*. See *Bush* v. *Martin,* 224, F. Supp. 509 (1966).

In treating the federal system as a multiple-level political system, it is necessary to recognize that demands may come not only from individual citizens or private groups, but also from local authorities. A city council delegation will frequently show up in Washington to demand better housing, airport subsidies, or grants-in-aid in many other forms. The same is true of other authorities acting upon the state or national level.[41] Legislation regarding water control, conservation, or expansion of districts may be sponsored and fought for by water district authorities, legislators, mayors, or governors. Thus, in employing a systems approach we must recognize that demands may flow from one political system to another via the authorities of the systems.

There are currently 3448 governmental units in Texas. Through the reserved power of the state, Texas has created these units, establishing the regimes and erecting the authority roles. The people within the jurisdiction of each unit elect the authorities. The relationship among the units is established by the state through legislation. Cooperation between some of the units (e. g., the city officials and the school board) may be informal, but it is often decisive in determining the outputs of each. In some cases, the output of one unit may be based upon the output of another; for example, the demands made by the authorities of the water district may be directly related to the actions taken by the Commissioners Court of two or more counties. City and county authorities are likely to maintain cooperation and informal communication so that each will know what the other is doing and be able to present the other with demands.

Texas, like other states, has a great variety of local governmental units. Although school districts are reducing their number through consolidation, special districts are increasing theirs. These special districts are highly specialized, single-function, governmental units. Their clientele is usually narrowly defined, but may range over a large geographic area. In some cases, the creation of special districts results from federal laws, such as housing and urban renewal legislation, or from demands upon the legislature from a single group. A listing of the districts illustrates the diversity of this governmental arrangement. The types and numbers of special districts in Texas are: Comal County Water District (1), Conservation and Reclamation (99), Drainage (56), Hospital (42), Housing (208), Levee Improvement (34), Navigation (25), Noxious Weed Control (3), Old Galveston Quarter (1), Rural Fire Protection (4), Soil and Water Conservation (190), and Water Improvement (339).

---

[41]More research could be done on authorities acting as pressure groups at all levels of government. For some recent work directly related to the point, see Daniel J. Elazar, *The American Partnership; Intergovernmental Cooperation in the Nineteenth Century* (Chicago: University of Chicago Press, 1962); and Roscoe C. Martin, *The Cities and the Federal System* (New York: Atherton Press, 1965).

To summarize, because Texas is but one of many state subsystems within the federal system, both the federal government and those of each of the states are major features in the environment of Texas politics—articulating wants, creating stresses, and forcing Texans to respond. By the same token, because Texas possesses many local subsystems, the state contains within itself the sources of significant political inputs. Out of the social, economic, and political milieu that constitutes the environment of Texas politics flow the conflicts the polity must regulate. Let us now examine how supports and demands are organized in that process of regulation.

# POLITICAL INPUTS: ORGANIZING SUPPORTS AND DEMANDS IN TEXAS

*PART TWO*

# 3

# Mobilizing Political Supports

As with any polity, the relationship of the Texas political system to its environment may be described in a number of ways. For reasons discussed in Chapter 1, we find it helpful to think of the political system as a set of interactions that facilitate responses to changes in the environment; through those responses, political inputs, appearing as demands upon governing officials, are converted into outputs. However, the demands arising in the environment frequently conflict with one another, and before the political system can resolve the differences effectively, the polity must have the support of a substantial number of its citizens. Without that support, policies are not accepted as legitimate, are often ignored, and may be actively disobeyed. Indeed, in the absence of support the very existence of the political system is endangered.

The constitutional structure of the Texas political system, despite amendments to the 1876 Constitution, has gone largely unquestioned for almost a century. Furthermore, there have been no periodic revolts against the occupants of political offices in that structure. On the other hand, there has been no evidence of widespread popular approval of all aspects of Texas government. From time to time, for example, Texans have turned out of office one set of elected rulers in preference for another; yet, policy-makers have continued to process demands into outputs without serious interruption. And, despite sundry amendments since 1876, the regime's constituted rules and structure, described in the last chapter, have been successfully used to resolve policy conflicts. There has been at least a minimal commitment among Texans to living together in political community, thus maintaining a viable state of the Union.[1] In this chapter we shall examine the types of support Texans extend to their political officials, institutions, and state—the context within which the interests discussed in the next chapter present political demands.

# POLITICAL ATTITUDES, PARTIES, AND PARTICIPATION IN TEXAS

Support for a political system—at least beyond the passive support that reflects mere apathy—comes from citizens either acting on behalf of the system or holding positive attitudes toward it.[2] We shall describe three areas in which favorable actions and attitudes are manifested toward the Texas polity—the political culture, political parties, and political participation.

### THE POLITICAL CULTURE OF TEXAS

We said in Chapter 1 that political culture is that aspect of a state's environment that encompasses what people know, believe, and feel about politics. Put another way, political culture is the particular pattern of attitudes people have toward political action. And, we suggested, in a state as diverse as Texas we might expect to find several such attitude patterns. If there are several distinct political subcultures in Texas, they probably reflect the state's sectionalism—the tying together of segments of the state "with bonds of shared economic and social interests."[3] Thus, in examining the political culture of Texas, we need to consider regional configurations as well as attitudinal ones. First, therefore, we will examine the extent of regionalism in Texas, and then designate the major ways in which Texans orient themselves to government.

## Regionalism in Texas

Most serious analyses of Texas stress that the state possesses a variety of climatic conditions, terrains, river systems, and vegetation groupings,

---

[1]For a discussion of the objects of political support—authorities, regimes, and political community—see David Easton, *A Systems Analysis of Political Life* (New York: John Wiley & Sons, Inc., 1965), pp. 171-219.

[2]*Ibid.*, p. 159.

[3]Daniel J. Elazar, *American Federalism: A View from the States* (New York: Thomas Y. Crowell Co., 1966), p. 79.

which, when taken together, form distinctive geographic regions. Associated with these regions, it is further stressed, are socioeconomic patterns and regional loyalties that leave their mark on the political map of Texas.[4] For students of the Texas political system, then, regional analysis poses three questions: (1) Are there indeed distinctive regions of Texas? (2) To the extent that regionalism exists, what socioeconomic features are related to each region? (3) If socioeconomic configurations match regional breakdowns, can we identify any regional patterns of political attitude that would lead us to conclude that Texas is a state of multiple political subcultures?

There is no universal agreement on what the various geographic regions of Texas are. Generally, however, accounts of Texas regionalism include at least the following: (1) *East Texas*, a region of red clay soil, largely forested with pines, extending westward from the Louisiana border north of Houston to an area approximately east of Dallas. (2) *Central Texas*, which includes several subregions—an east-central area of postoak, blackjack, elm, hickory, and walnut trees, dotted with small farms; a central subregion of black soil, where small farms give way to larger tracts that were once the plantations of Texas; and a west-central subregion of rolling hills that gradually extend to plains and thence to the Hill Country rising north of San Antonio, a rocky and hilly area of gullies and draws. (3) *West Texas*, a region extending to the New Mexico border of dry climate and high plains including the Caprock, the Rolling Plains, and the Permian Basin. (4) *The Panhandle*, the grassy, high-plain area jutting into Oklahoma and bordering on New Mexico. (5) *South Texas*, the mesquite- and brush-covered region generally south of San Antonio, with a subregion of mild climate and citrus production extending along the reaches of the Rio Grande. (6) The *Gulf Coastal Plain*, the sea-level region extending inland along the Gulf of Mexico and including a subregion in southeast Texas along the Sabine River. (7) The *Trans-Pecos*, a rugged region that extends west of the Pecos across the Santiago and Davis mountains to the subregion of the southwest and New Mexico. (8) *North Texas*, which lies along the Red River in a section roughly north of Dallas and Fort Worth.

When we examine the economic and social patterns of Texas we find that their spatial demarcations correspond closely to these geographic regions. The United States Bureau of the Census, for example, divides the entire nation into 13 economic regions composed of contiguous counties whose economic environments (types of crops, industries, housing facilities, population densities, etc.) are essentially similar. Each region is further divided into subregions, and each subregion into state economic areas.

---

[4]See, for example, David Nevin, *The Texans* (New York: William Morrow & Company, Inc., 1966), pp. 48–56.

Texas consists of 19 state economic areas, with uniform economic environments, that roughly parallel the geographic regions described above.[5]

But the regions of Texas are more than homogeneous geographic and economic divisions. Each region's social composition is fairly uniform as well. If we examine ethnic composition, for instance, we note that Mexican-Americans are located predominately in urban areas or in the counties of the Gulf Coastal Plains, South Texas and the Southwest.[6] Texas blacks reside predominantly in urban counties or in East Texas. If we turn to the socioeconomic status of Texans, we find again that regional differences are apparent. Figure 3-1 displays the counties of Texas according to 1960 census data on the types of occupations predominant in the county, the average educational attainment of county residents, and the county's median family income.[7] Upper-class counties are those which rank above the state average on all three criteria; middle-class counties are those which rank above the state average on any one of the three criteria; and lower-class counties are below the state average on all three.

Clearly, lower-class counties predominate in the Gulf Coastal Plains, South Texas, and particularly East Texas (the "land of poverty").[8] Central Texas is more prosperous, having several middle- and upper-class counties. West Texas and the Panhandle are regions of comparative affluence, with a concentration of upper-class counties. The exceptions to the regional patterns occur primarily in the metropolitan centers, where Harris, Travis, Dallas, Tarrant, and Wichita counties are ranked as upper-class. Indeed, although most sociodemographic patterns in Texas roughly follow regional divisions, the major exceptions usually lie within metropolitan areas. Since in the 1970s the population of metropolitan Texas will be greater than in

---

[5]Donald J. Bogue and Calvin L. Beale, *Economic Areas of the United States* (Glencoe, Ill.: The Free Press, 1959). The general question of regionalism in comparative state politics is discussed in Raymond E. Wolfinger and Fred I. Greenstein, "Comparing Political Regions: The Case of California," *American Political Science Review*, LXIII (March 1969), 74–85; Ira Sharkansky, "Regionalism, Economic Status and Public Policies," *Social Science Quarterly*, 49 (June 1968), 9–26; and "Regional Patterns in the Expenditures of American States," *Western Political Quarterly*, 20 (December 1967), 955–71; Charles R. Adrian, "Regional Analysis in Political Science," *Social Science Quarterly*, 49 (June 1968), 27–32.

[6]R. L. Shrabanek, *A Decade of Population Change in Texas* (College Station, Texas: Texas Agricultural Experiment Station, Texas A & M University, 1963), pp. 9–10.

[7]The occupational and educational measures are, more specifically: (1) the percentage of the employed labor force in occupations classified in the 1960 census as professional, technical, proprietary, and managerial; and (2) the percentage of individuals, 25 years of age and older, with 8 or more years of schooling; (3) the median family income. See U.S. Bureau of the Census, *United States Census of Population: 1960*, Vol. I, *Characteristics of the Population*, Part 45, *Texas* (Washington, D.C.: Government Printing Office, 1962).

[8]Ruth A. Allen, *East Texas Lumber Workers: An Economic and Social Picture, 1870-1950* (Austin: University of Texas Press, 1961), p. 3.

*Mobilizing Political Supports* 49

Upper-Class Ranking Counties

Middle-Class Ranking Counties

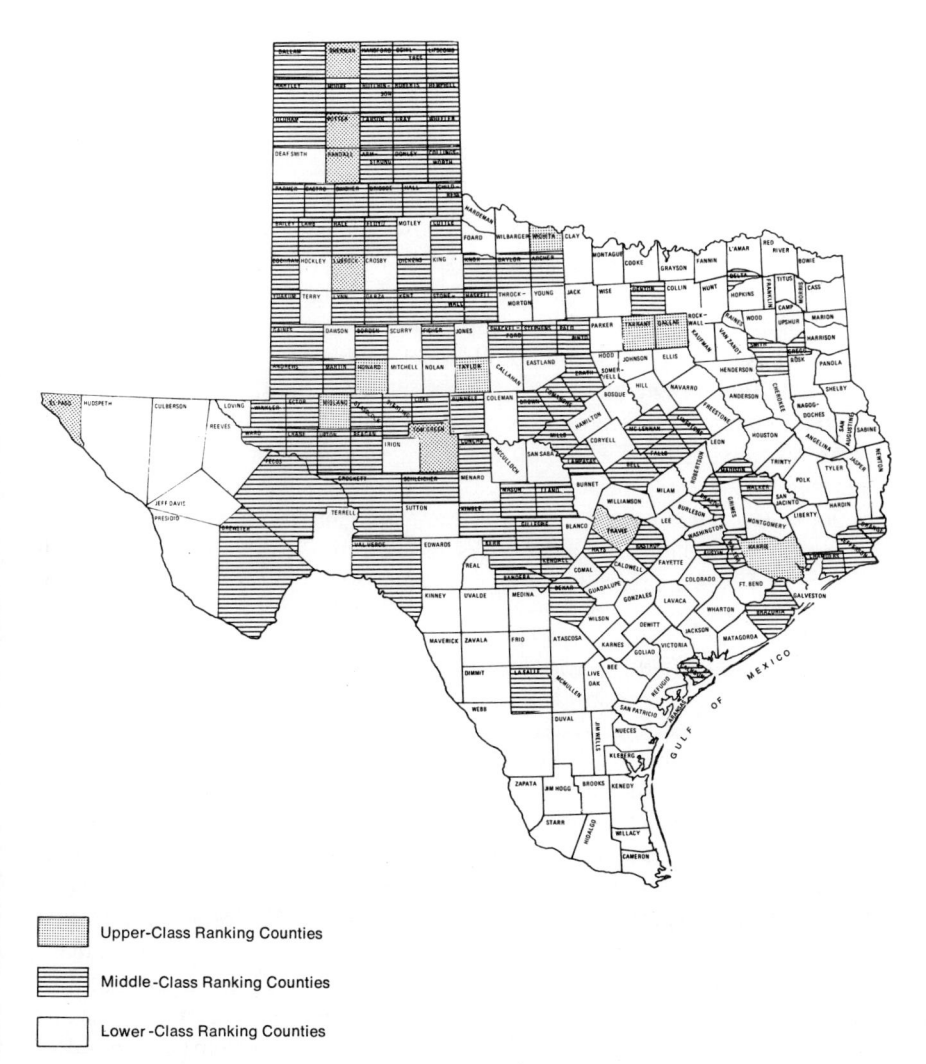

Lower-Class Ranking Counties

FIGURE 3-1. Social class ranking of Texas counties, 1960.

nonmetropolitan counties, further diversification of subcultures is likely, with rural, urban, suburban, and metropolitan forces overriding the traditionally important regional factors in Texas politics.

In the decades before the 1970s at least, the regions of Texas differed from one another not only in geographic, economic, ethnic, and social characteristics, but in political attitude as well. Attitudes toward racial segregation in public schools illustrate these regional differences. In 1956, Texans voting in the Democratic primary had an opportunity to express themselves in a ballot referendum as favoring or opposing the desegregation of public schools. One study analyzing the results of that vote revealed that resistance to desegregation was lowest in prosperous regions (as measured by median family income), such as the grassy high plains of the Panhandle; in regions where the Mexican-American culture predominated, such as the Trans-Pecos and the Valley, where the population is more than 50 percent Latin; and, naturally, in regions with sizable black minorities.[9]

For the present, then, we shall accept the proposition that, as a state political system, Texas possesses multiple political subcultures, and that in some respects, at least where attitudes are related to the "shared economic and social interests" in a section, these political subcultures approximate regional divisions of the state. Do Texans hold any political attitudes, however, that transcend regional loyalties and permit us to speak of the political culture of Texas apart from regional subcultures?

## The Political Orientations of Texans

Political scientists have made relatively little investigation of the political cultures of the various states and none at all of the political culture of Texas.[10] However, a recent analysis of the nature of American federalism as viewed by the states provides a useful approach to the types of political orientations (knowledge, beliefs, and values) that we might expect to find in Texas.[11] That study contends that the political culture of the United States is itself a synthesis of three major political subcultures—the individualistic, moralistic, and traditionalistic. In the *individualistic* political culture, government is popularly conceived of as a marketplace in which policies emerge from the bargaining of individuals and groups acting out of self-interest. Governmental intervention in matters regarded as private

---

[9]Werner F. Grunbaum, "Desegregation in Texas: Voting and Action Patterns," *Public Opinion Quarterly*, 28 (Winter 1964), 604–14.

[10]See, however, Samuel C. Patterson, "The Political Cultures of the American States," *Journal of Politics*, 30 (February 1968), 187–209.

[11]Elazar, *American Federalism*, pp. 79–116.

(e.g., business enterprise) is limited, politics is viewed only as a tool for individual social and economic improvement, political parties seek to control office primarily to distribute rewards and favors to party loyalists, political activity is carried on by professional politicians, and the citizen acquiesces to policy decisions but takes no active part in shaping them. People in a *moralistic* political culture believe that government exists to promote and maintain a shared public interest (the good society) rather than separate private interests. Since government exists to advance the shared interest of all citizens, it is believed that every citizen should participate, that government should intervene into private matters to advance the public good, and that political parties should command the loyalties of citizens to the extent that they, the parties, contribute to community improvement rather than dispense patronage. Finally, a *traditionalistic* political culture is based on a paternalistic and elitist conception of government. Political power is reserved for a small and self-perpetuating elite with a "right" to govern because of family or social position, the role of government is to preserve the established social order, the preference is for a single political party (often divided into factions) that merely fills public positions with persons sympathetic to elitist policies, and the average citizen is not expected to participate in politics (not even to vote), but to accept passively the will of the ruling oligarchy.

Admittedly, these three types of political subcultures are oversimplifications of much more complex and contradictory realities. Yet, as Figure 3-2 indicates, the scheme permits us to sketch the general patterns of political orientation across the United States. Interestingly enough, and as we would expect from our discussion of Texas regionalism, Texas possesses a combination of two of these subcultures: traditionalism and individualism. East Texas, for example, is traditionalistic; Central and South Texas are dominated by traditionalism, but have strains of individualism; and West and Trans-Pecos Texas are predominantly individualistic, with traditionalistic elements. The general pattern in Texas, however, is an amalgam— traditionalism spiced with individualism (a pattern also found in Oklahoma, Kentucky, West Virginia, and Florida).[12]

What aspects of Texas politics warrant the designation traditionalistic-individualistic? Certainly one we must include is the tendency, remarked upon by many observers of the Texas scene, for Texans to emphasize material self-interest above notions of the public good—an individualistic orientation. One writer notes this tendency in describing the "action culture" of Texas, where "the key is movement, accomplishment, building; action, not reflection; the builder, not the thinker." In this action culture, "the builder is supreme and his tool is money." And, in keeping with the

---

[12]Elazar, *American Federalism*, p. 108.

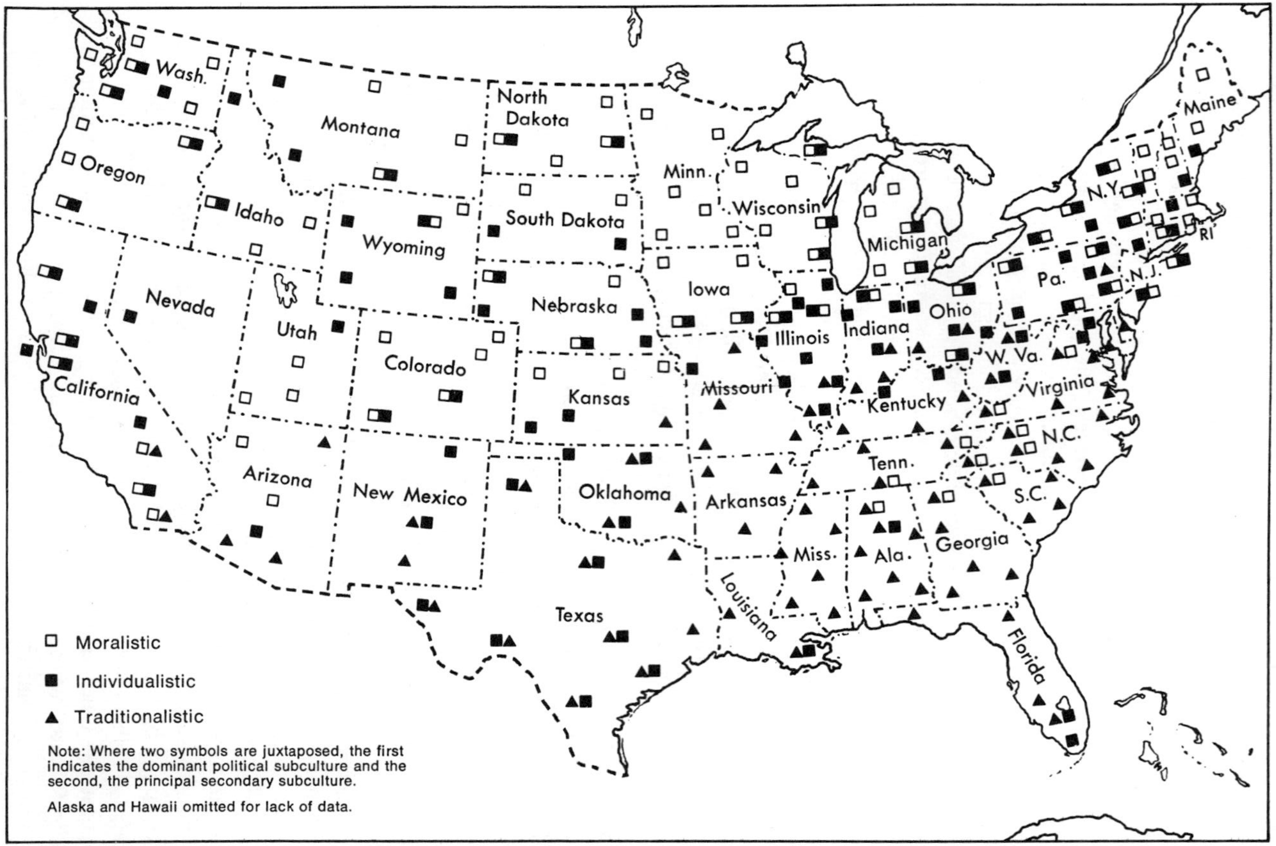

FIGURE 3-2. The distribution of political cultures within the states

Adapted from Daniel J. Elazar, *American Federalism: A View from the States* (New York: Thomas Y. Crowell Company, 1966), p. 97. Copyright © 1966.

individualistic, not moralistic, strain of the political culture, "Texans are often generous individually, but rarely collectively," since "individual generosity is the individual's business" but "generosity systematized through government helps those whom the builder disdains anyway, people who can't or, as he suspects, won't produce."[13]

Although impressions of one writer, of course, do not define the culture of a state, there are other tendencies in Texas politics that lead us to suspect that the designation of traditionalistic-individualistic, albeit an oversimplification, is accurate. In both traditionalistic and individualistic political cultures, for example, citizens are generally indifferent to political issues. Surveys of Texas adults indicate this is the case in the Lone Star State. Indeed, one of the major orientations of Texans is not to concern themselves with politics at all! In 1967 a statewide sample of 1058 adult Texans were asked questions concerning a variety of issues being considered by the Texas Legislature that year: tuition at state-supported colleges, salaries for public school teachers, penalties for persons convicted of crimes, and qualifications for automobile drivers. Although almost all Texans had opinions on at what age drivers should be licensed, few had any knowledge or awareness of the other issues. When asked whether tuition levels in Texas were higher or lower than in other states, 53 percent declared they did not know and another 31 percent responded incorrectly; when asked how much teachers' salaries should be increased, 43 percent had no opinion; 13 percent had no opinion on prison penalties.[14]

Moreover, in traditionalistic-individualistic political cultures policymaking is left to the politicians; private citizens seldom know or care about the results of, for instance, legislative sessions. In 1969, following one regular and two special sessions of the Texas Legislature, 1021 Texans were questioned about which actions of the legislature they could remember and whether they liked or disliked the actions taken. Aside from a tax increase (recalled by one-third of the respondents), very few of the specific actions could be remembered by more than a very few persons. In line with the individualistic pattern, most complaints were leveled at legislative actions supporting government intervention in private, material areas. As an indication of the extent to which acceptance of governmental action in a traditionalistic culture derives more from passive acquiescence than informed support, 72 percent of the respondents could not think of anything the legislature did that they liked, while 50 percent could think of nothing it did that they disliked.[15]

Such surveys, of course, do not prove that Texans are any more or less informed, concerned, or passive about public affairs than are citizens of

---
[13] Nevin, *The Texans*, pp. 182–83.
[14] "The Texas Poll," *Polls*, III (Winter 1967), 93-94.
[15] "The Texas Poll," *The Dallas Morning News*, October 12, 1969.

other states. Yet, in a state marked by an action orientation in material endeavors, one would expect the citizenry to be more aware of what governing officials are doing that might pertain to those endeavors. That Texans are not more aware lends some support to the notion that an attitude of "action, not reflection" is characteristic of the traditionalistic-individualistic pattern. Other characteristics of Texas politics that fit that pattern are the one-party dominant system (split by factions), low levels of electoral participation, and the overrepresentation of established interests in making political demands (see Chapter 4).

## THE TEXAS PARTY SYSTEM

A political party is an organization of enduring yet frequently conflicting interests that mobilizes support for candidates seeking public office in competitive elections; through its representatives in official positions, a political party strives to control policy-making. A party system consists of all the political parties in a polity competing for control and thus is but one of the many subsystems of the more inclusive political system. We are interested in three major aspects of the party system in Texas—the number and structures of parties in the system, the role of the parties in recruiting the political leaders of Texas, and factional alignments.

## Party Organizations

Any discussion of the party system in Texas must specify the number of parties that compete for control of governmental offices. This is a complicated task that involves more than simply counting the number of parties listed on the ballot in any single election. In determining the extent of party competition, we must know how many party organizations consistently provide alternative slates of candidates in elections and how frequently alternative parties are successful in winning public office.

Political scientists employ a variety of measures to determine the degree of competition between parties in the states and to gauge the dominance of one party or another in state politics. Figure 3-3 compares the various states according to levels of party competition in 1962-1968 for lower houses of the state legislature, upper houses of the state legislature, and governorships. The comparison is based upon the degree of success of the majority party, be it Democrat or Republican. Thus, in the battle for lower house seats, Alabama and Arkansas are among those states with the least interparty competition while Michigan and New Jersey are among those with the most. Figure 3-3 shows that during the decade under investigation, Texas proved to have one of the least competitive party systems of

*Mobilizing Political Supports* 55

**Lower Houses**

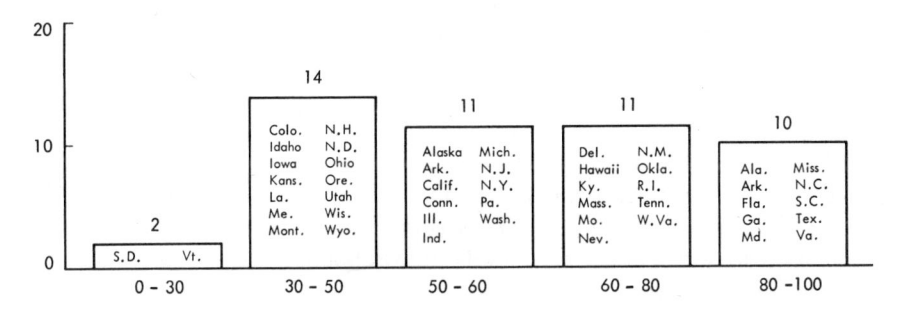

| Range | Count | States |
|---|---|---|
| 0–30 | 2 | S.D., Vt. |
| 30–50 | 14 | Colo., N.H., Idaho, N.D., Iowa, Ohio, Kans., Ore., La., Utah, Me., Wis., Mont., Wyo. |
| 50–60 | 11 | Alaska, Mich., Ark., N.J., Calif., N.Y., Conn., Pa., Ill., Wash., Ind. |
| 60–80 | 11 | Del., N.M., Hawaii, Okla., Ky., R.I., Mass., Tenn., Mo., W.Va., Nev. |
| 80–100 | 10 | Ala., Miss., Ark., N.C., Fla., S.C., Ga., Tex., Md., Va. |

Percentage of Total Seats Held by Democrats, 1962–1966

**Upper Houses**

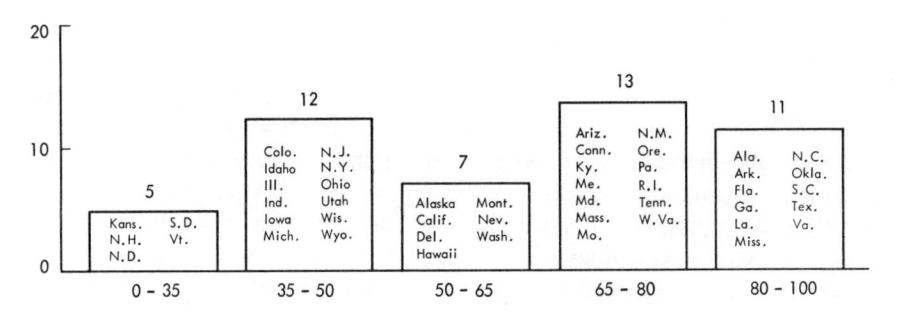

| Range | Count | States |
|---|---|---|
| 0–35 | 5 | Kans., S.D., N.H., Vt., N.D. |
| 35–50 | 12 | Colo., N.J., Idaho, N.Y., Ill., Ohio, Ind., Utah, Iowa, Wis., Mich., Wyo. |
| 50–65 | 7 | Alaska, Mont., Calif., Nev., Del., Wash., Hawaii |
| 65–80 | 13 | Ariz., N.M., Conn., Ore., Ky., Pa., Me., R.I., Md., Tenn., Mass., W.Va., Mo. |
| 80–100 | 11 | Ala., N.C., Ark., Okla., Fla., S.C., Ga., Tex., La., Va., Miss. |

Percentage of Total Seats Held by Democrats, 1962–1966

**Governors**

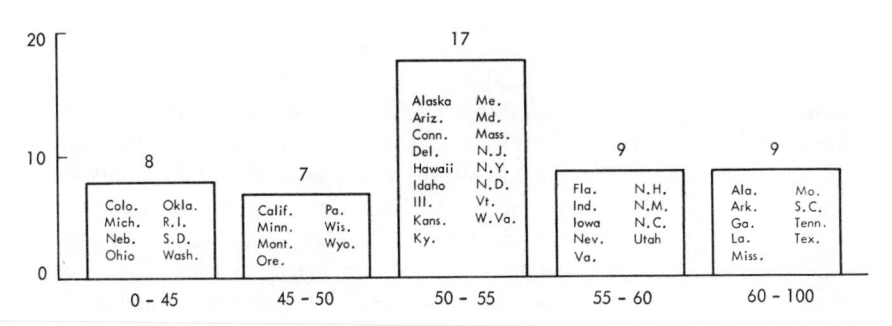

| Range | Count | States |
|---|---|---|
| 0–45 | 8 | Colo., Okla., Mich., R.I., Neb., S.D., Ohio, Wash. |
| 45–50 | 7 | Calif., Pa., Minn., Wis., Mont., Wyo., Ore. |
| 50–55 | 17 | Alaska, Me., Ariz., Md., Conn., Mass., Del., N.J., Hawaii, N.Y., Idaho, N.D., Ill., Vt., Kans., W.Va., Ky. |
| 55–60 | 9 | Fla., N.H., Ind., N.M., Iowa, N.C., Nev., Utah, Va. |
| 60–100 | 9 | Ala., Mo., Ark., S.C., Ga., Tenn., La., Tex., Miss. |

Average Democratic Percentage in Votes for Governor, 1962–1966

FIGURE 3-3. Distribution of states by level of interparty competition, 1962-1966
*Source:* Thomas R. Dye, *Politics in States and Communities* (Englewood Cliffs, New Jersey: Prentice-Hall, Inc. © 1969), p. 98. Reprinted by permission.

all states. Texas thereby qualifies as a *one-party* state, one in which public offices and elections are dominated by a single party; in a *two-party* state, the division of popular votes in elections and control of offices is reasonably close.

As any resident of Texas knows, the one party that dominates Texas politics is the Democratic party. How Texas compares with other states with regard to one-party dominance is shown in Figure 3-4, which indicates the degree of Democratic and Republican control of the states from 1962- 1966. As one might suspect, Texas is one of the most Democratic-dominated of the states at all three levels—lower house, upper house, and votes for governor. The Democratic monopoly in Texas is even more apparent when seen against an over-all state index of party competition, 1946 to 1953, measuring the average percentage of the popular vote won by Democratic gubernatorial candidates, the average percentage of seats in the state senates held by Democrats, the average percentage of seats in the state houses of representatives held by Democrats, and the percentage of all terms for governor, senate, and house in which Democrats had control. A high average percentage (90 or above) indicates a one-party, Democratic-dominant state; an average of 70 to 89 percent indicates a modified Democratic dominance; and an average of 30 to 69 percent indicates a two-party state. Using this scheme, Texas ranks fifth among the Democratic-dominant states with an average of 96 percent, following South Carolina, Georgia, Louisiana, and Mississippi, in that order.[16] In the past, then, Texas has been one of the extreme examples of one-party, Democratic-dominant politics—a fact in keeping with the proposition that Texas exhibits a predominantly traditionalistic political culture.

The patterns of the past, however, may yield to change in the future. In the late 1960s Texas Republicans made continuing challenges to Democratic dominance. Although not matching their most notable success of electing a United States Senator (John Tower) in 1961 and reelecting him in 1966, Republicans captured two state senate seats and nine house seats in 1968, and the Republican candidate for Governor in 1968 received 43 percent of the total vote, considerably above the average percentage for Republicans in previous years. Therefore, although Texas will remain basically a one-party state in the foreseeable future, it may in time shift gradually from one-party Democratic dominance to modified Democratic dominance.

Several studies have endeavored to identify the factors associated with vigorous, two-party competition and one-party politics. It has been found that, in general, two-party states have a higher percentage of their population in urban areas than do one-party states, and that one-party,

---

[16]Austin Ranney, "Parties in State Politics," in *Politics in the American States*, eds. Herbert Jacob and Kenneth N. Vines (Boston: Little, Brown & Co., 1965), pp. 64-66.

*Mobilizing Political Supports* 57

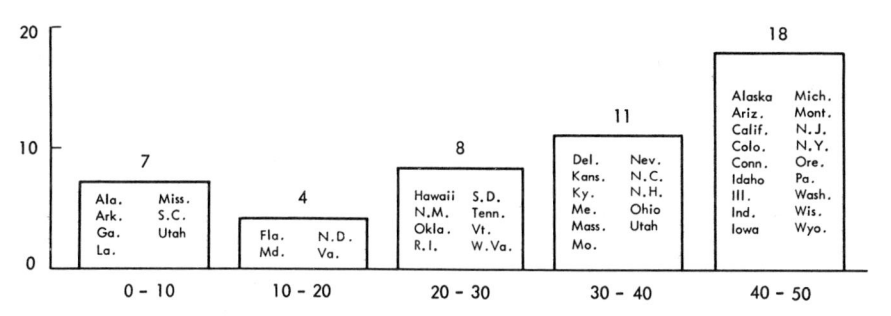

**Lower Houses**

| 0-10 | 10-20 | 20-30 | 30-40 | 40-50 |
|---|---|---|---|---|
| 7 | 4 | 8 | 11 | 18 |
| Ala. Miss.<br>Ark. S.C.<br>Ga. Utah<br>La. | Fla. N.D.<br>Md. Va. | Hawaii S.D.<br>N.M. Tenn.<br>Okla. Vt.<br>R.I. W.Va. | Del. Nev.<br>Kans. N.C.<br>Ky. N.H.<br>Me. Ohio<br>Mass. Utah<br>Mo. | Alaska Mich.<br>Ariz. Mont.<br>Calif. N.J.<br>Colo. N.Y.<br>Conn. Ore.<br>Idaho Pa.<br>Ill. Wash.<br>Ind. Wis.<br>Iowa Wyo. |

One Minus the Percentage of Seats Held by the Majority Party, 1962-1966

**Upper Houses**

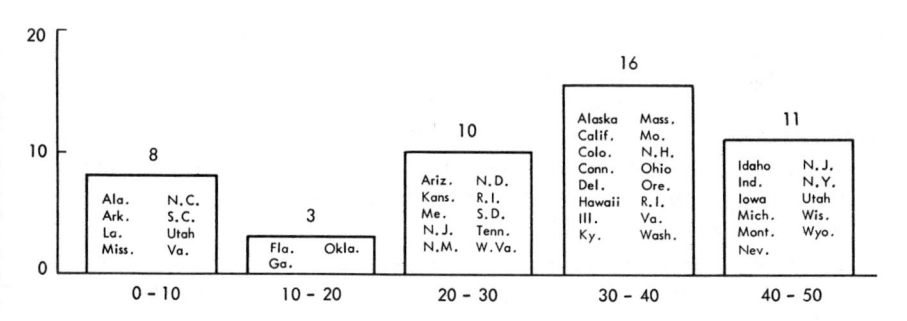

| 0-10 | 10-20 | 20-30 | 30-40 | 40-50 |
|---|---|---|---|---|
| 8 | 3 | 10 | 16 | 11 |
| Ala. N.C.<br>Ark. S.C.<br>La. Utah<br>Miss. Va. | Fla. Okla.<br>Ga. | Ariz. N.D.<br>Kans. R.I.<br>Me. S.D.<br>N.J. Tenn.<br>N.M. W.Va. | Alaska Mass.<br>Calif. Mo.<br>Colo. N.H.<br>Conn. Ohio<br>Del. Ore.<br>Hawaii R.I.<br>Ill. Va.<br>Ky. Wash. | Idaho N.J.<br>Ind. N.Y.<br>Iowa Utah<br>Mich. Wis.<br>Mont. Wyo.<br>Nev. |

One Minus the Percentage of Seats Held by the Majority Party, 1962-1966

**Governors**

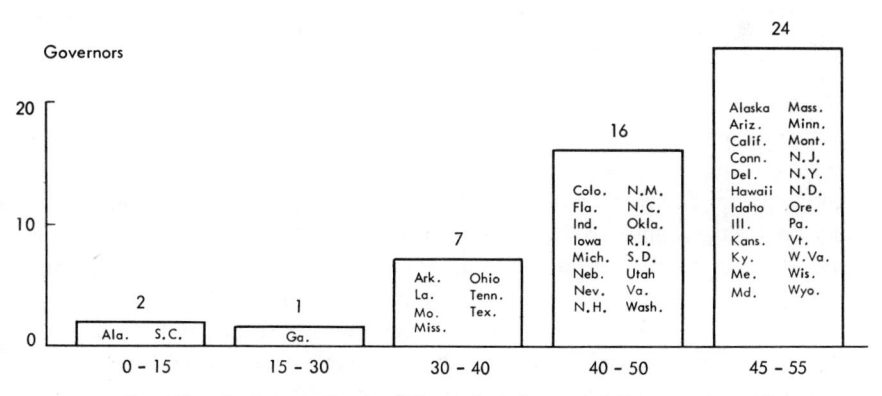

| 0-15 | 15-30 | 30-40 | 40-50 | 45-55 |
|---|---|---|---|---|
| 2 | 1 | 7 | 16 | 24 |
| Ala. S.C. | Ga. | Ark. Ohio<br>La. Tenn.<br>Mo. Tex.<br>Miss. | Colo. N.M.<br>Fla. N.C.<br>Ind. Okla.<br>Iowa R.I.<br>Mich. S.D.<br>Neb. Utah<br>Nev. Va.<br>N.H. Wash. | Alaska Mass.<br>Ariz. Minn.<br>Calif. Mont.<br>Conn. N.J.<br>Del. N.Y.<br>Hawaii N.D.<br>Idaho Ore.<br>Ill. Pa.<br>Kans. Vt.<br>Ky. W.Va.<br>Me. Wis.<br>Md. Wyo. |

One Minus the Average Margin of Victory in Gubernatorial Elections, 1962-1966

FIGURE 3-4. Distribution of states by Democratic and Republican control of state government, 1962-1966

*Source:* Thomas R. Dye, *Politics in States and Communities* (Englewood Cliffs, New Jersey: Prentice-Hall, Inc. © 1969), p. 103. Reprinted by permission.

Democratic-dominant states have markedly lower median family incomes and a significantly higher percentage of blacks than do two-party states.[17] It is questionable, however, that changes solely in the sociodemographic characteristics of Texas would produce a decline of one-partyism. A study of two-party voting in all counties of the United States in the 1960 presidential election revealed that social, economic, and demographic factors had little relation to the degree of two-party competition. In Texas, the only such factors even slightly associated with the absence of two-party competition in the 1960 election were the functional illiteracy of a county's population and its percentage of nonwhite residents. The study concluded that other factors such as internal party organization and leadership, legal considerations, campaign strategies, and accidents of political history are just as important as sociodemographic characteristics in explaining the presence or absence of two-party competition.[18]

The proposition that the type of party system in a state is related to the internal organization and leadership of each party suggests that to understand the party system of Texas we need to turn our attention to party structure. Party structure refers to the stable pattern of relationships existing between party leaders and followers. It thus includes the nature of party membership (who are the followers), the agencies responsible for ongoing party activities (that relate leaders to followers), and the effective exercise of influence (who are the leaders).

In all states, membership in political parties is determined both by law and by practice. In Texas, party membership is largely a legal determination (basically in pursuance of the Terrell Election Law of 1905). A citizen does not register his party preference, but is considered a member of a political party if, as a qualified voter, he participates in the primary of that party or, should there be no primary, attends the party's precinct convention. Since party primaries and precinct conventions occur every two years, a Texan can change his party membership frequently. However, being a legally designated Democrat or Republican need not affect either the Texan's voting loyalties or his long-term partisan predilections. Hence, a lifelong Democrat may vote in the primary of the Republican party (and thus be legally considered a Republican), yet vote for Democrats in the general election. By the same token, it is not uncommon for self-styled and legally designated Democrats to vote Republican in presidential and senatorial elections in Texas. This is one reason why it is impossible to develop tightly knit, hierarchical party structures in Texas: party memberships are simply too ambiguous and loyalties too shifting.

---

[17]*Ibid.*, pp. 68-69.

[18]Charles M. Bonjean and Robert L. Lineberry, "The Urbanization-Party Competition Hypothesis: A Comparison of All United States Counties," *Journal of Politics*, 32 (May 1970), 305-21.

Since party membership is legally defined in Texas, it is possible to obtain a rough picture of the differences between the followers of the two parties by noting the types of people that vote in Democratic or Republican primaries. Unfortunately, data on primary voters throughout the state are not available. However, we can draw a limited profile of the membership of each party by utilizing data based upon a random sampling of 4123 qualified voters in Texas' largest metropolis, Harris County (Houston), in 1964 and 1013 qualified voters in 1966. We hardly expect Harris County to be representative of all of Texas, but these data illustrate at least that the two major parties do appeal to different clienteles. Comparing voters in the Republican and Democratic primaries of those years on the basis of four sociodemographic factors reveals that Democratic followers tend to be male, between 30 and 60 years of age, white (but with a sizable proportion of blacks and a smaller percentage of Mexican-Americans), and distributed fairly equally between professional-managerial and blue collar workers. Republican party members tend to be female, between 21-30 and 40-50 years of age, white, and in professional-managerial occupations.

On paper, political parties in Texas appear to be structured into permanently organized hierarchies, with party activists at each level subordinate to those immediately above them. At the lowest level, the voting precinct, the party official is the precinct chairman; he is elected by the party membership in the primary or in precinct conventions in the absence of a primary. The strength of the party's grass roots organization is in the precinct chairman's hands, and he tends those grass roots by registering and mobilizing voters for elections, exerting control over his precinct's conventions, and responding to the demands of the party candidates, officials, and members. In most instances an effective precinct chairman can influence the outcome of a campaign. Precinct chairmen are frequently relied upon by candidates, even in party primaries where chairmen frequently only feign neutrality. A survey of 63 out of 74 candidates for the state legislature from Harris County in 1966 revealed, for example, that 46 felt that precinct chairmen had been of assistance in their campaigns.[19] And, as indicated by a 1968 study of precinct activity in the gubernatorial primary, effective precinct organization improves the chances of a candidate's success in areas where his party or faction is in a minority.[20]

The party's precinct chairmen in a county comprise the party's county executive committee. That committee is responsible for the conduct of

---

[19]*Legislative Recruitment in Texas: The Case of Harris County* (Houston: Public Affairs Research Center, University of Houston, 1967).
[20]Richard W. Murray, "The Impact of Partisan Organization in the Transitional Political Environment: The Case of Harris County, Texas," paper delivered at the meetings of the Southwestern Political Science Association, Houston, Texas, April 3, 1969.

party primaries and the county convention. The chairman of the county executive committee is immediately superior to the precinct chairman and generally the key party functionary at the local level. Elected either in the party primary or by the county convention, he is responsible for delivering electoral majorities to party and preferred factional candidates and for keeping a tight control over the county organization on behalf of the ruling party faction.

The agency speaking for the party at the statewide level is the state executive committee, which consists of a chairman, vice-chairman, and one man and one woman from each senatorial district in the state. Members are selected by the state convention from persons nominated by delegates from the senatorial districts, and there is frequent in-fighting over their selection between rival factions and county organizations. This intraparty conflict provides the opportunity for dominant interests at the state level (usually representing the governor, in the case of the Democrats) to mobilize support in the convention for their own nominees. Moreover, by controlling the state executive committee, established interests (see Chapter 4) can influence the conduct of the primaries, the state convention, party propaganda, and the role of the state party in national politics.

Paralleling each of these levels of party structure are devices for injecting token popular representation into the conduct of party affairs. These are the precinct, county, district, and state conventions. Precinct conventions are open to all legally designated party members, and each level of convention thereafter selects delegates to the next higher one. Thus, the faction that controls the precincts is in a good position to control other levels of the organization. In an organization as fragmented as the Democratic party, however, intense rivalries at each level convert party conventions as much into ideological battlegrounds as deliberative or decision-making bodies. In all but presidential election years, the state convention is held in September, substantially after the May primaries, to certify the party's candidates for the general election, select the state executive committee, etc. In presidential election years, an earlier convention is held before the September fracas to select a national committeeman, committeewoman, and delegates to the national party convention. The September convention then has the added task of approving or disapproving the national party's presidential candidate.

As is the case with party followers, we have no precise indicators of the types of people who serve as party workers in the organizations. Again, our available data are limited to party activists in Harris County in 1966, some with previous experience as precinct leaders, county chairmen, and delegates to state conventions or national presidential nominating conventions. Generally, these party activists are male, middle-aged, college educated (usually with professional degrees), and in professional or white collar occupations.

They are predominantly white, but blacks and Mexican-Americans are of course represented in the precinct leadership of their respective ethnic neighborhoods.

Given the multiplicity of local organizations (they exist in each senatorial district, county, and precinct), there are strong tendencies toward fragmentation in both of the major parties of Texas. In the Democratic party, the long-term retention of the governorship has given the party a central focus of leadership even in the face of seemingly fratricidal intraparty conflict. With the support of major interests in the state, the Governor has been able to exercise a continuing influence over party affairs. In the Republican party in recent years, leadership has been exercised by the more attractive and successful candidates of the party and by state party officials with access to national Republican leaders. Should the Republicans elect a governor, it would raise serious organizational problems for both parties. The centrifugal tendencies in the Democratic party would be intensified with the loss of the governorship as a pivotal point, and a Republican governor would be forced to vie for influence in his party with the state chairman, the national committeeman, and the relatively few Republican statewide and local office-holders.

## Party Nominations

A principal rationale for the existence of political parties is that they are agencies through which we recruit individuals to govern. Parties serve as such agencies by nominating candidates and mobilizing support for them in competitive elections. Key state offices in Texas have traditionally been won by candidates of the Democratic party. Indeed, with the exception of bids for the governorship and a few legislative seats, Republicans have not even contested Democrats for control of Texas government. Although Republicans evidenced renewed interest in elections for state offices in the late 1960s (contesting elections for legislative seats in Harris and Dallas counties and for governor), the Democratic nomination in one-party Texas is still tantamount to election in many regions. Thus, by nominating candidates who eventually occupy state offices, the Democratic party is a major mobilizer of supports for both the regime and the authorities in the Texas political system.

Both of the major political parties in Texas nominate candidates through the primary (a party must do so if its candidate for governor in the most recent election received 200,000 or more votes) rather than in a party convention. Party nominees are chosen by party members through majority vote in primaries held the first Saturday in May; in the event that no candidate receives a majority, a second primary one month later allows party members to choose between the two candidates receiving the most votes in the first primary. Party nominees then square off in elections held the following November. The primaries are administered by the parties (that is, the parties print the ballots, assign the polling places, count the votes, etc.) and financed by them (principally through filing fees levied upon candidates.) Since candidates must file for their party's primary early in the election year, a candidate runs for office from early spring until fall. Hence, a public official serving only a two-year term may spend as much as one-third of that term seeking reelection.

We do not know a great deal about what motivates a person to seek his party's nomination in a primary, but we can make a few guesses on the basis of the research at hand. Generally, a candidate can be a "self-starter" (one whose candidacy stems from personal aspirations, ideals, conscience, etc.) or he can be "recruited" (stimulated to run by the party, an official, a private group, friends, family, etc.).[21] Despite their interest in having successful nominees, Texas political parties seldom exercise a leading role in recruiting candidates. In a study interviewing 13 candidates seeking party nominations for legislative seats in the Austin area in 1962, for example, nine of the candidates were classified as self-starters and one as motivated by friends; only three (one Democrat and two Republicans) had been recruited to run by their party organizations.[22] Similarly, in another study of 63 persons seeking nominations for state legislative offices from the Harris county area in 1966, fewer than one-third felt their party had even remotely influenced their decision to run in the primary.[23] If we ask what types of people seek party nominations, the same studies indicate that the aspirants are generally similar to one another: typically, they have had several years of experience in politics, are in professional or business occupations, are in their mid-twenties and early thirties, have had college educations, and are usually male, Protestant, and white.

There is one major area of Texas politics where parties play an even smaller role, or no role at all, in the selection of public officials. This is at the local level, where elections to municipal offices are nonpartisan. A nonpartisan election is one in which candidates run without party affiliation or designation. Interestingly enough, Texas law permits party nominations in city elections, but rarely do parties exercise the option. This is doubtless a carry-over from an earlier era of Democratic dominance when lack of opposition obviated the need for the party to designate candidates; the party organization thus became inactive and moribund in local elections, and

---

[21]Lester Seligman, "Political Recruitment and Party Structure," *American Political Science Review*, LV (March 1961), 77-86.

[22]David M. Olson, *Legislative Primary Elections in Austin, Texas: 1962* (Austin: Institute of Public Affairs, The University of Texas, 1963), p. 16.

[23]*Legislative Recruitment in Texas*.

"no party" politics grew into the widespread institution of nonpartisan elections.[24]

## Party Factions

We have remarked on the tendency for Texas political parties to be torn by factional strife, and have noted that factionalism is a characteristic of single parties that dominate traditionalistic political cultures. A faction is a group within a political party, organized in a reasonably durable alliance and united in the pursuit of a common objective opposed to the aims of competing partisan groups. The common objective uniting a faction's members may be economic, regionalistic, or ideological, or directed toward the candidacy of a particular personality. In Texas, major factions—the conservatives and the liberals—compete for control within the Democratic party, and until only recently the Republicans were more characteristic of a factional than a party organization.

V. O. Key's classic account of party politics in the southern states, written slightly over two decades ago, observed that "in Texas the vague outlines of a politics are emerging in which irrelevancies are pushed into the background and people divide broadly along liberal and conservative lines." Instead of people grouping themselves around colorful figures for the pursuit of temporary gain, or dividing over racial matters, the "Lone Star State is concerned about money and how to make it, about oil and sulfur and gas, about cattle and dust storms and irrigation, about cotton and banking and Mexicans." Consequently, "a modified class politics seems to be evolving, not primarily because of an upthrust of the masses that compels men of substance to unite in self-defense, but because of the personal insecurity of men suddenly made rich who are fearful lest they lose their wealth."[25]

There is some doubt that the Texas party system has evolved entirely as Key predicted. For one thing, factions based largely upon the personal magnetism of single candidates still emerge. Indeed, given the efforts of some candidates to build personal followings by employing the image-making techniques of public relations firms, survey research, and television, we might expect personal factions to appear even more frequently in the future.[26] Moreover, as we shall see in our discussion of electoral participation patterns, voting alignments in Texas do not necessarily parallel the divisions of social class. Yet, in the 1950s and 1960s the factional align-

---

[24]David M. Olson, *Nonpartisan Elections: A Case Analysis* (Austin: Institute for Public Affairs, The University of Texas, 1965), pp. 5-10.

[25]V. O. Key, Jr., *Southern Politics in State and Nation* (New York: Alfred A. Knopf, 1949), pp. 254-55.

[26]Michael Mansfield, "Professional Public Relations and Political Power in Texas" (Master's thesis, North Texas State University, Denton, Texas, 1970).

ments in the dominant Democratic party did reflect ideological outlooks tied to differing economic interests.

The conservative Democratic faction has generally reflected the interests of the upper middle-class population, that is, of white, native-born Texans, usually in white-collar or commercial occupations. This is not to say that conservative sentiment is missing among lower income groups—one study, for example, reveals that several counties with relatively low median family incomes frequently support conservative candidates.[27] Still, conservative Democratic strength is usually strongest in the more prosperous counties of North Texas, the Panhandle, far West Texas in the southern plains subregion, and the Hill Country. And, the high-income, white-collar precincts of selected metropolitan areas (Houston, Dallas, Amarillo, Midland, and Lubbock) are centers of the voting strength of the conservative faction.

The liberal Democratic faction took root in the Populist era of the late 1800s, and by the 1960s was emphasizing the interests of the less dominant elements in Texas—the economically disadvantaged, racial-ethnic minorities (blacks and Mexican-Americans), labor unions, blue-collar workers, younger Texans, and intellectuals. From what was once a voting strength restricted to East Texas, a cluster of counties in the Panhandle, and the rolling area of the North, liberal Democrats have extended their appeal and received sizable blocs of support in South Texas, the Southeast, and the low-income, blue-collar, ethnically diverse precincts of such metropolitan counties as Dallas, Tarrant (Fort Worth), Travis (Austin), Wichita (Wichita Falls), Potter (Amarillo), McLennan (Waco), Harris (Houston), Bexar (San Antonio), Nueces (Corpus Christi), and Galveston.

In the 1960s, as we have seen, the Republican party in Texas was not sufficiently competitive to warrant calling Texas a two-party state. Yet, the appeal of the Republicans by the close of the decade put them on a par with either the conservative Democrats or the liberal Democrats. In fact, it is likely that a rough division of political loyalties would now find one-third of the voters in each of the three camps in statewide elections. Armed with this new strength, the Republicans in the last decade developed genuine chances for victory by (1) attracting liberal Democrats disenchanted with a conservative Democratic nominee—as happened in 1966, when liberal Democrats aided the reelection of U.S. Senator John Tower over Attorney General Waggoner Carr, or by (2) converting a sufficient number of conservative Democrats to win elections in formerly conservative areas—as happened, again in 1966, in the election of Representative George Bush in the Texas 7th congressional district. By the same token, the emergence of the Repub-

---

[27]James R. Soukup, Clifton McCleskey, and Harry Holloway, *Party and Factional Division in Texas* (Austin: The University of Texas Press, 1964).

licans on a competitive level with conservative Democrats offered liberal Democrats the possibility of holding the balance of power between contending conservative candidates—as exemplified again by the 1966 reelection of Senator Tower.

At the start of the 1960s, Republican strength was centered in parts of the Panhandle and those counties of the Hill Country with high proportions of Germanic stock. But new voting strength was added as a result of militant organization in suburban Texas combined with an appeal to the emerging class of professionally and technologically employed Texans, to middle-class females active in civic affairs, to migrants from other states, and to relatively prosperous white-collar workers. It was metropolitan Texas (especially Lubbock, Amarillo, Dallas, Houston, Fort Worth, Midland, and Odessa) that contributed to Texas Republicanism.

Thus, the 1960s—considered from the perspective of economically based partisan factions—had several discernible characteristics. First, the one-party system evolved (some would say degenerated) not into a two-party politics of social class, but into the tri-factional arrangement in which conservatives, divided between two parties, outnumbered liberals. Second, the controlling factions of both major parties were conservative and representative of the old and new Texas prosperity (not the impoverished), the suburbs (not the central cities or rural regions of poverty), and the white population (not the black or Mexican-American). Third, traditional regional alignments in the one-party system yielded gradually to the press of urbanization, with both liberal Democrats and Republicans establishing factional bases in the major metropolises. To see how the above social factors—class, ethnicity, and urbanism—relate to the organization of political supports in Texas, we must examine their impact upon electoral participation.

## ELECTORAL PARTICIPATION IN TEXAS

Citizens relate to state political systems in various ways—by gathering political information, discussing politics, campaigning, writing to officials, contributing money to candidates, joining political parties, attending political rallies, running for office, and voting. The types of participation and the numbers of people involved differ from state to state, partly because of the differences in the political cultures of state governments: whereas moralistic political cultures (e.g., Idaho and Utah) urge participation, traditionalistic ones (e.g., Arkansas and Mississippi) encourage relatively little political involvement.[28] Texans rarely do anything more in politics than

---

[28]Lester W. Milbrath, "Political Participation in the States," in *Politics in the American States*, eds. Jacob and Vines, p. 25.

vote, and, on the average, only about half of the eligible electorate vote in state elections. Since voting is the most common—though hardly pervasive—form of mass political activity, let us consider the voting turnout and alignments in Texas.

## Voting Turnout in Texas

Each state has age and residency requirements that citizens must meet in order to be eligible to vote. In most states the age requirement is 21 years, but Georgia and Kentucky permit 18-year-olds to vote, and Alaska and Hawaii permit 19- and 20-year-olds, respectively. The normal residence requirement is one year in the state, but 13 states require only six months and Mississippi demands two years. Thus, the Texas requirements—21 years of age or older, and one-year residence in the state—fit the general pattern. United States citizenship is, of course, another requirement, and idiots, lunatics, county-supported paupers, and certain felons are ineligible to vote in Texas.

But eligibility alone does not qualify a person to vote; he must still *register* his eligibility with election officials. Registration may be permanent (the voter registers, and his name remains on the list until he leaves the voting district) or periodic (he must reregister at specified intervals). Since the periodic system requires the voter to take the initiative and reregister from time to time (except in states such as Idaho that send registrars from house to house), many otherwise eligible voters do not participate in elections simply because of the inconvenience, nuisance, and difficulty of registration. In traditionalistic Texas, the periodic system obtains, with registration carried on yearly over the four-month period between October 1 and January 31, well before the citizen's political interest is stimulated either by the party primaries in May or the general elections the following November. There is evidence that the Texas registration process disadvantages certain elements of society; members of minority groups, the young, the unskilled, the less educated, and the poor register in disproportionately smaller numbers than other elements of the eligible electorate. Since these are the people least likely to vote for the conservative Democrats who usually win state offices in Texas, the registration process that filters them out of the electorate actually constitutes another form of political support for the conservative Democratic regime and officials.[29]

---

[29]Clifton McCleskey and Dan Nimmo, "Potential, Registered, and Actual Voters," *Social Science Quarterly*, 49 (June 1968), 103-14; Dan Nimmo and Clifton McCleskey, "Impact of the Poll Tax on Voter Participation," *Journal of Politics*, 31 (August 1969), 662-99; Harry Holloway and David M. Olson, "Electoral Participation by White and Negro in a Southern City," *Midwest Journal of Political Science*, X (February 1966), 99-122.

The qualified voter in Texas, then, is one who meets the citizenship, age, and residency requirements of Texas and then certifies his eligibility through registration. In 1968 there were 5,534,277 Texans who were eligible to participate in state and national elections; of that total, 4,072,000 proceeded to qualify through registration—3,532,000 of the 4,884,765 eligible whites, and 540,000 of the 649,512 eligible blacks. Yet, of the more than 4 million qualified voters, only 3,079,396 voted in the 1968 presidential election and even fewer—2,916,352—voted in the gubernatorial contest. Thus, of every ten eligible voters in Texas in 1968, three could not vote for Governor because they had not registered and another two, roughly, who were qualified did not exercise their franchise. In other words, only about one out of every two Texans eligible to vote in the 1968 elections actually did so.

The 1968 count, however, was not unusually low for Texas. In fact, Texans turned out to vote that year in greater proportions than normal. Only 40-50 percent of Texans voted in the presidential elections of the 1960s, and 40-47 percent in gubernatorial races held the same years. But only 20-30 percent voted in gubernatorial elections held in the "off years" when there was no presidential race. Indeed, turnout in the Democratic party's gubernatorial primary has only once (in 1956) exceeded 30 percent of the eligible electorate!

Is the depressed rate of electoral participation peculiar to Texas or more widespread? In gubernatorial elections between 1960-1968, Texas ranked in the lowest one-third of all states in the average percentage of the voting-age population casting votes. States with turnout rates lower than Texas were Georgia, Mississippi, South Carolina, Tennessee, and Virginia; states on the same level as Texas were Florida, Iowa, Kentucky, Oklahoma, and Maryland. The pre-1960 picture was much the same: in a ranking of 48 states according to average turnout in gubernatorial and senatorial elections in non-presidential years in the 1950s, Texas was 44th with an average turnout of 13.6 percent (compared to the highest-ranking state, Idaho, with 64.6 percent).[30] In the traditionalistic political culture of Texas, then, a depressed level of electoral participation is indeed a tradition.

There are a number of factors associated with the low rate of citizen participation in Texas politics. For one, only since 1967 has Texas had a system of free registration; until then the state required citizens to pay a poll tax in order to vote. Even the periodic registration that currently exists is restrictive, but less so than the earlier poll tax arrangement. Second, people are more likely to qualify and vote when they believe the election outcome will make a difference in public affairs. The lack of interparty competition in general elections and the dominance of the conservative faction in state-

---

[30]Milbrath, "Political Participation in the States," p. 40.

wide Democratic primaries leaves some Texans with the feeling that meaningful participation is impossible. Third, and related to the second factor, it is frequently hard for Texans to see how voting in elections gives them any real voice in policy-making; access to policy-makers is more frequently facilitated through membership in prosperous private groups (see Chapter 4). Fourth, Texas political parties have not engaged in any grass-roots programs vigorous enough to stimulate involvement among citizens; aside from the liberal Democratic faction, no group has made any serious effort to involve those people who are virtually nonmembers of the Texas political community—the blacks, Mexican-Americans, poor, and young.

Finally, the state's cultural expectations do not and never have dictated that citizens *should* influence system outputs by participating in political inputs; the standard has been for Texans to respond to the decisions of the political system rather than for political officials to respond to the views of citizens. Such expectations have had their impact upon Texans' (particularly minority Texans') attitudes toward participation. Surveys of political attitudes in Texas in 1969 reveal that 46 percent of the blacks and 40 percent of the Mexican-Americans interviewed had little belief that year that their actions as citizens could affect governmental decisions. Only 27 percent of the whites felt so ineffective. Moreover, a majority of the blacks (52 percent) and over one-third of the Mexican-Americans had strong feelings of political alienation; their attitudes toward government were withdrawn and hostile. One-fourth of the whites were alienated to the same degree.[31] Thus, rules, parties, factions, cultural expectations, and attitudes combine to depress electoral participation in the Lone Star State.

## Partisan Voting Alignments

Earlier we noted the patterns of regional strength for each of the three factions in Texas politics—conservative Democrats, liberal Democrats, and Republicans. We also alluded to the tendency for certain sociodemographic factors (class, race-ethnicity, and urbanism) to be associated with the composition of each faction. Here we want to explore a final facet of the relationship between these sociodemographic factors and partisan supports for the Texas political system: the place of sociodemographic considerations in voting alignments.

Ideally, to investigate the impact of any influence on voter behavior one should observe the activity of individual voters, question them regarding their political sentiments, and gather information about their social and

---

[31]Clifton McCleskey and Bruce Merrill, "The Political Behavior of Mexican-Americans in Texas: A Preliminary Report," paper delivered at the meetings of the Southwestern Political Science Association, Dallas, Texas, March 28, 1970.

economic background. To do this, political scientists have employed survey research as the appropriate tool in a number of studies of the political behavior of the national electorate and many state and local electorates,[32] but rarely have they conducted statewide opinion surveys in Texas of sufficient scope to provide the type of information that can contribute to our knowledge of Texas politics. Commercial firms frequently conduct surveys (the Texas Poll, for example), but the range of concerns involved is narrow and the data sometimes unreliable. Moreover, both political scientists and commercial firms are occasionally reluctant to part with their masses of data.

Consequently, with survey research into the attitudes and behavior of Texas voters not available, we shall employ an alternate technique, aggregate analysis, to study voter alignments. This involves comparing the voting returns in each Texas county with selected sociodemographic characteristics of that county. Thus, although we cannot compare the social and economic characteristics of individual Texans with their voting preferences, we can make assertions about the types of counties returning pluralities or majorities for liberal Democrats, conservative Democrats, or Republicans. To do so, we make use of a measure which permits us to describe the extent to which county sociodemographic characteristics and vote totals are related and the extent to which variations in one are associated with variations in the other. That measure is the coefficient of correlation, and it has a range of -1 to +1. If, for example, as a person grows taller he also grows heavier, we say his height and weight are positively correlated; a correlation coefficient of .800 say, would indicate a high positive correlation, and a coefficient of only .200, a slight one. If, however, the person loses weight as he grows taller, the correlation coefficient comparing inches and pounds would be negative—say -.400, indicating a moderate association. If there is no association between the two factors—that is, if changes in one are unrelated to changes in the other—the correlation coefficient would be .000. In our discussion of voting alignments in Texas, we are interested in reporting the correlations between selected sociodemographic characteristics and voting totals for the 254 counties of the state.

We are concerned primarily with three sociodemographic factors—social class, race-ethnicity, and urbanism. For each of these factors we have gathered the following data on each of the 254 counties:[33]

1. Social Class
   a. An occupation ratio consisting of percentage of the labor force in

---

[32]See Angus Campbell, Philip E. Converse, Warren E. Miller, and Donald E. Stokes, *The American Voter* (New York: John Wiley and Sons, 1960); and Alvin Boskoff and Harmon Zeigler, *Voting Patterns in a Local Election* (Philadelphia: J. B. Lippincott Co., 1964).

[33]U.S. Bureau of the Census, *United States Census of Population: 1960*, Vol. I, Part 45.

each county in the following 1960 census categories: "craftsmen foremen, and kindred workers," "operatives and kindred workers," "farm laborers and farm foremen," and "laborers, except farm and mine." The lower the percentage, the higher the occupational class of the county.
   b. An education ratio consisting of the percentage of persons aged 25 and over in each county in 1960 who had only eight years of schooling or less. The lower the percentage, the higher the educational class of the county.
2. Race-Ethnicity
   a. A "racial" ratio consisting of the percentage of each county's population in 1960 in the "nonwhite" category, which includes "native parentage," "foreign or mixed parentage," or "foreign born."
   b. A parentage ratio consisting of the percentage of each county's residence of "foreign or mixed" parentage, regardless of color.
3. Urbanism
   a. An urban ratio consisting of the percentage of each county's population in 1960 residing in urban areas.
   b. A female labor-force ratio consisting of the percentage of females in each county in 1960 classified as being in the labor force. (High percentages of employed women are characteristic of urban areas.)[34]

Finally, because of our interest in the growing support for the Republican party in Texas in the 1960s, we also employ a measure (a migration ratio) telling us what percentage of each county's population in 1960 had migrated to the county from out of the state in the previous decade.

Figure 3-5 contains the correlation coefficients of each of the sociodemographic measures with two sets of elections. The first set of correlations is based upon the percentage of the total votes in each county cast for each Republican presidential candidate over the last two decades and for the Republican senatorial candidates in 1961, 1964, and 1966. The second set of correlations reflects conservative Democratic strength and is based upon the percentage of each county's vote cast for the conservative Democrat in the 1964 Democratic gubernatorial primary and for conservative Preston Smith (vs. liberal Don Yarborough) in the 1968 second Democratic gubernatorial primary (held after the first primary, in which none of the candidates received a majority).

We must exercise caution in interpreting the data in Figure 3-5. At the time of the analysis only 1960 census data were available, and since the census is taken only once every ten years, more current data will not be available until well into the 1970s. In Texas, a state undergoing rapid social

---

[34]Eshref Shevky and Wendel Bell, *Social Area Analysis* (Stanford, Calif.: Stanford University Press, 1959).

**FIGURE 3-5** Correlations Between Voting Alignments in Recent Elections and Indices of Socio-demographic Factors

| | GOP Presidential Vote 1948 | GOP Presidential Vote 1952 | GOP Presidential Vote 1956 | GOP Presidential Vote 1960 | GOP Presidential Vote 1964 | GOP Presidential Vote 1968 | GOP Senatorial Vote 1961 | GOP Senatorial Vote 1964 | GOP Senatorial Vote 1966 | Conservative Democratic Vote, Senatorial Primary '64 | Conservative Democratic Vote, Governor's 2nd Primary 1968 |
|---|---|---|---|---|---|---|---|---|---|---|---|
| GOP Presidential Vote 1948 | | | | | | | | | | | |
| GOP Presidential Vote 1952 | .71 | | | | | | | | | | |
| GOP Presidential Vote 1956 | .74 | .82 | | | | | | | | | |
| GOP Presidential Vote 1960 | .47 | .78 | .71 | | | | | | | | |
| GOP Presidential Vote 1964 | .38 | .64 | .63 | .80 | | | | | | | |
| GOP Presidential Vote 1968 | .47 | .69 | .54 | .72 | .61 | | | | | | |
| GOP Senatorial Vote 1961 | .67 | .82 | .77 | .83 | .77 | .68 | | | | | |
| GOP Senatorial Vote 1964 | .38 | .67 | .59 | .78 | .92 | .66 | .76 | | | | |
| GOP Senatorial Vote 1966 | .46 | .67 | .65 | .76 | .83 | .57 | .78 | .83 | | | |
| Conservative Democratic Vote, Senatorial Primary '64 | .28 | .53 | .57 | .56 | .62 | .29 | .46 | .61 | .55 | | |
| Conservative Democratic Vote, Governor's 2nd Primary 1968 | .05 | .28 | .09 | .28 | .15 | .39 | .13 | .26 | .15 | .30 | |
| Occupation | -.01 | -.05 | .14 | -.12 | -.05 | -.20 | -.05 | -.11 | -.13 | .16 | -.15 |
| Education | .15 | -.17 | -.03 | -.44 | -.44 | -.36 | -.30 | -.49 | -.41 | -.10 | -.22 |
| Nonwhite | .27 | -.07 | .14 | -.28 | -.16 | -.29 | -.05 | -.25 | -.15 | -.09 | -.34 |
| Foreign Parentage | .46 | .25 | .19 | -.16 | -.17 | .12 | .12 | -.14 | -.10 | -.09 | -.05 |
| Urban Residence | .15 | .06 | .13 | .13 | .15 | .15 | .22 | .19 | .31 | -.01 | -.21 |
| Women in Labor Force | .29 | .30 | 31 | .38 | .37 | .35 | .40 | .40 | .47 | .15 | -.06 |
| Migration | -.03 | .12 | .05 | .24 | .30 | .23 | .25 | .27 | .26 | .05 | -.08 |

and economic changes, we expect 1960 sociodemographic variables to have less relevance to voting statistics with each successive election. Hence, the most valid relationships in the data center upon the presidential election of 1960 and the senatorial election of 1961. We should also keep in mind that our sociodemographic indicators of class, race-ethnicity, and urbanism are not the only ones that might have been selected. We have used a limited number primarily for illustrative purposes. Finally we must emphasize that we are dealing with the aggregate, not individual, characteristics of all the voters in a county unit.

Given these limitations, what can we make of the array of correlations in Figure 3-5? First, we are struck by the fact that the correlations between the indicators of our three sociodemographic factors and votes cast for Republicans or conservative Democrats are uniformly low. We thereby infer that in most instances the relationship between the sociodemographic factors and voting alignments is negligible. This indicates the probable importance of other, more directly political, factors in shaping Texas voting patterns—e.g., variations from county to county in the strength of parties and factions; voters' long-term political attitudes vis-à-vis candidates, issues, and parties; the styles and strategies of campaigns; the legal restrictions placed upon voting populations; and voters' memberships in business, labor, ethnic, agrarian, and other organizations. Indeed, the multiple correlation of all our sociodemographic factors taken together with voting data in each election ranges from .44 in 1956 to .75 in 1964. If we square the multiple coefficient correlation, we obtain a coefficient of determination; this statistic tells us roughly what proportion of the variation in Republican or conservative Democratic strength from county to county can be attributed solely to the combination of all our sociodemographic factors. Since the highest coefficient of determination (1964) is only .56, we must conclude that at least 44 percent of the variation in voting patterns is attributable to other social, political, or legal factors.

Despite their slightness or lowness, however, the correlations do go in the expected directions. With regard to class, for example, the smaller the proportion of lower-class occupations in a county, the greater the degree of voting support for Republican presidential and senatorial candidates and for conservative Democrats. Similarly, the higher the percentage of a county's residents with eight or fewer years of schooling, the smaller the voting strength for Republicans or conservative Democrats. These relationships, weak though they seem, do lend credence to the earlier assertion that liberal Democratic strength differs along class lines from that of Republican and conservative Democratic strength.

By the same token, the voting strength of Republicans and conservative Democrats in the elections of the 1960s is inversely related to the percentage of nonwhites in the counties. Note, however, that the relationship between the parentage ratio and voting preferences is mixed, probably reflecting a pattern in which liberal support among Mexican-Americans cancels conservative (Republican and Democrat) support among other ethnic groups such as the Texas Germans.

The urban areas of the South have been major bases for the resurgence of Republicanism. Our data give us some reason to make this assertion. First, while the correlations are again low, the higher the percentage of a county's population residing in urban areas, the greater the Republican proportion of the total county vote, regardless of the election. Furthermore, the most substantial correlations between sociodemographic variables and voting are those between the percentage of females in each county's labor force and the proportion of votes cast for Republican candidates. Although working women come from all social classes, those in the middle class in Texas have been particularly receptive to Republican appeals. Our correlations probably reflect this tendency. Finally, it should be noted that the vote for conservative Democrats is negatively correlated with urban residence, in part indicating the tendency for liberal Democrats to appeal to the minority elements in the more metropolitan of the urban counties.

It might also be asserted that the growing support for the Republican party in Texas results as much from the migration of Republicans into the state as from the conversion of conservative Democrats or the indoctrination of new voters. The low correlations between our migration measure and Republican patterns, although positive, aid us little in choosing between the alternative explanations. A correlation between 1970 migration data (when available) and electoral patterns of the late 1960s will be more revealing.

We should not turn from Figure 3-5 without commenting upon the correlations between elections. It is interesting, for example, that county-by-county Republican strength in 1948 is not as highly correlated with later Republican strength as are the Republican figures for 1952. People have suggested that the candidacy of Dwight Eisenhower in 1952 brought many persons into the Republican party who remained to support Republican candidates for President and U.S. Senator in later elections. Our data tend to support this view with regard to Texas. For a similar example of "vote by association" note the high correlation (.920) in the county-by-county support for presidential candidate Barry Goldwater and senatorial candidate George Bush in 1964; although hardly unexpected (both were Republicans running on the same ticket), the relationship is striking. It is also noteworthy that the pattern of support for conservative Democrat Gordon McClendon running against liberal Ralph Yarborough in the 1964 Democratic senatorial primary correlates well with the voting support given Republican Bush in the November senatorial election. Although it is impossible to infer it from our data, one wonders about the extent to which disenchanted conservative Democrats support Republicans in the general election if the conservative of their own party fails to achieve nomination. A concluding observation about our inter-election correlations is warranted: the high to very high correlations between Republican percentages in the elections of the 1960s may indicate that the basic pattern of county-by-county voting strength has been formed and that Republicans will solidify their bases of support in the 1970s. Any conclusions respecting this proposition, of course, must await the election returns of the coming decade.

## SUPPORT POLITICS IN TEXAS

Retracing our path through the preceding discussion, what generalizations are we justified in making regarding the supports for the Texas political system contained in the political culture, political parties, and electoral participation patterns of the state? As far as the cultural factor is concerned, we have discussed two tendencies in Texas politics—the long-term, but possibly decreasing, role of regionalism and the more overarching presence of a traditionalistic-individualistic political culture. With regard to political parties we have seen that Texas has a faction-ridden, single-party system that exhibits a few tendencies to emphasize social class distinctions, but more often than not excludes the truly lower social classes. And as for electoral participation, we have observed that it engages fewer than half of those Texans eligible to take part, because of restrictive registration requirements, the absence of vigorous two-party competition, social conditions, a tradition of popular indifference to politics, and the seeming irrelevance of popular elections to policy-making.

With respect to these observations, we can only hope that political scientists will undertake systematic research to test their validity. For the present, however, we must accept the fragmentary data and impressions reviewed in this chapter and conclude that the general orientations of Texans toward government *support* the major characteristics of the political regime —policy-making in the hands of a relatively small set of politically active leaders; a tri-factional, one-party-dominant party system; minimal participation by the mass of citizens in political affairs (even in elections); a reluctance for government to intervene in private sectors of life (especially respecting economic interests); and a generally passive acceptance of the existing social and political order by most citizens.

There are various types of political systems. One might speak, for example, of the political system embedded in a culture where all citizens are expected to take an active part in declaring their support for the governmental regime and its officials. In such a "citizen" culture, members avidly define their demands, articulate them, and express them to policy-makers. But in Texas this is not the case. Active political support flows from the upper- and middle-class elements of Texas society; the less prosperous

Texans acquiesce to the way things are rather than display concerned involvement or active participation in affairs of state. They are less "citizens" than they are "subjects" of the political system.[35] And in a polity where "subjects" predominate, political orientations, political parties, and popular elections constitute supports, not demands, in the political system. Where, then, do the demands arise? To what demands do policy-makers respond? And, if policy-makers do not respond to popular demands, yet rely upon passive popular supports, how democratic is the political system? These are questions relevant to our discussion in the following chapter.

---

[35]Gabriel A. Almond and Sidney Verba, *The Civic Culture* (Princeton: Princeton University Press, 1963), Chap. 1.

# 4

# Presenting Political Demands

Were all inputs to the political system supportive, there would be no need for government. The function of the polity is to respond to and adjust the conflicting demands originating in the environment. In the Texas political system, the principal source of conflicting demands is the multitude of interest groups represented in Austin. In this chapter we examine these suppliers of political demands, their expectations, their techniques, and their success in maintaining dominance in what has been alleged to be the "Texas Establishment."

## INTEREST GROUPS AND DEMAND POLITICS

Our emphasis in the last chapter on the supportive functions served by ideological factions, parties, and the electoral system suggests that these activities are relatively ineffective in communicating and converting demands into policies. In many states, particularly Texas, interest groups supplement the efforts of voters, parties, and partisan factions in organizing political inputs. To see how this is so, let us look at the variety of interest-group activity in state political systems, and then focus specifically upon the political interests of Texas.

## INTEREST GROUPS IN STATE POLITICAL SYSTEMS

There is no unanimity among political scientists on the precise nature of interest politics, but a widely accepted notion defines an interest group as "any group that, on the basis of one or more shared attitudes, makes certain claims upon other groups in the society for the establishment, maintenance, or enhancement of forms of behavior that are implied by the shared attitudes."[1] In pressing their political demands, interest-group members may or may not interact with one another and establish a formal organization through which to represent themselves. In 1969, for example, a set of concerned Texas taxpayers, each member acting spontaneously as an individual, wrote and telephoned members of the Texas House of Representatives protesting a proposal to levy a sales tax on food items. Still other citizens collaborated with one another and organized demonstrations against the tax within the visitors' galleries of the House chamber. The measure failed by unanimous vote. The point is that political interests may, and frequently do, exist in the absence of formal organization. When an interest group does organize to press demands, the organization so formed constitutes a *pressure group*, "a collection of individuals who consciously band together, amalgamate their strength, consult on questions of organization strategy, and undertake action in pursuit of their goals."[2] It is the combined interaction of these groups as they attempt to influence policy-making that we label the *pressure system*, one of the many subsystems of a polity. The distinction between unorganized and organized interests is particularly significant in Texas because, as we shall see, the more effective interests have been those capable of organizing considerable resources in pursuit of specific goals.

A precise measurement of the presence of pressure politics in the various states is impossible. The best estimate comes from those states that require organizations seeking to influence legislation to register any lobbyists used for that purpose. In some states a substantial number of persons register on behalf of groups (534 in California and 779 in Kansas in 1961); in others there are only a handful (58 in Alaska in 1962).[3] But such figures grossly understate the extent of pressure activity, since many organizations freely ignore registration laws either because the laws themselves are vague or because they are totally unenforceable.

More important than the number of pressure organizations in state politics is the type of interest most commonly represented through the pres-

---

[1] David B. Truman, *The Governmental Process* (New York: Alfred A. Knopf, 1958), p. 33.

[2] Harmon Zeigler, *Interest Groups in American Society* (Englewood Cliffs, N. J.: Prentice-Hall, Inc., 1964), p. 30.

[3] *The Book of the States 1962-63* (Chicago: Council of State Governments, 1962), p. 86.

sure system. In virtually every state requiring registration of lobbyists, business interests are the most frequently represented by organized interests. In 1964 in New York, for example, 74 percent of the registered lobbyists represented business interests (either business associations or single corporations, as did 63 percent in South Dakota, 56 percent in Kentucky, and 52 percent in California. Texas is no exception. In the 1969 session of the Texas legislature there was approximately one registered lobbyist representing business interests for each member of the Texas House and Senate.

Despite the fact that pressure politics is common in all states, Americans generally do not regard organized activity as a preferred method for influencing governmental policy. In 1960, for instance, in a national survey measuring the reaction to alternate ways of preventing the passage of an unjust or harmful law, the sample of adults generally favored individual and informal means (such as contacting elected officials directly or working through informal groups) over action through organized groups. Yet, the same people perceived formal organization, when used by others, as an effective device for influencing legislation; in fact, 58 percent of the sample accepted the view that some persons and groups possess so much influence that the interests of the majority are often ignored. This paradox, if it is that, of people viewing pressure politics as effective, yet wishing to avoid organized activity, reflects in part the view held by many citizens throughout the country that pressure groups employ questionable and corrupt techniques for manipulating pliable state officials.[4]

But how really potent, in general, are pressure groups in the states? To answer this question we can marshal only the impressions, not the research, of political scientists. The single effort to measure the strength of groups in state politics appeared in 1954;[5] it was based upon a questionnaire sent to political scientists in each state, asking them to rate pressure groups in that state as strong, moderately strong, or weak. The guesses of political scientists resulted in 24 states (Texas among them) being classified as having strong groups, 14 as having moderately strong groups, and 7 as having weak groups (see Table 4-1). A later analysis utilizing the 1954 data attempted to estimate the extent to which pressure-group strength is associated with the presence or absence of meaningful competition between political parties in elections, the degree of unity displayed by party representatives voting in legislatures, and the economic development of the state as indicated by per capita income, urbanization, and industrialization.[6] That analysis con-

---

[4]Harmon Zeigler, "Interest Groups in the States," in *Politics in the American States*, eds. Herbert Jacob and Kenneth N. Vines, (Boston: Little, Brown and Co., 1965), pp. 102-103.
[5]Belle Zeller, ed., *American State Legislatures* (New York: Thomas Y. Crowell Co., 1954), pp. 190-91.
[6]Zeigler, "Interest Groups in the States," pp. 113-17.

cluded that interest groups tended to be stronger in one-party states than in competitive two-party states, in states lacking cohesive partisanship in their legislatures, and in the less affluent, largely rural, and agricultural states. If that is true, then the data we have examined in previous chapters on the Texas environment and party system would certainly lead us to expect strong pressure groups in Texas politics.

TABLE 4-1  Interest Group Strength in the States in the 1950s

| Strong | Moderately Strong | Weak |
| --- | --- | --- |
| Alabama | Delaware | Colorado |
| Arizona | Illinois | Connecticut |
| Arkansas | Kansas | Indiana |
| California | Maryland | Missouri |
| Florida | Massachusetts | New Jersey |
| Georgia | Nevada | Rhode Island |
| Iowa | New York | Wyoming |
| Kentucky | Ohio | |
| Louisiana | Pennsylvania | |
| Maine | South Dakota | |
| Michigan | Utah | |
| Minnesota | Vermont | |
| Mississippi | Virginia | |
| Montana | West Virginia | |
| Nebraska | | |
| New Mexico | | |
| North Carolina | | |
| Oklahoma | | |
| Oregon | | |
| South Carolina | | |
| Tennessee | | |
| Texas | | |
| Washington | | |
| Wisconsin | | |

Source: Based on data in Belle Zeller, ed., American State Legislatures (New York: Thomas Y. Crowell Co., 1954), pp. 190-91.
Note: Alaska, Hawaii, Idaho, New Hampshire, and North Dakota are not included.

One other set of relationships between interest groups and state politics will help us put the Texas pressure system in perspective. In examining pressure activity in the various states, distinct patterns emerge.[7] In rural, agricultural states, for example, where one party dominates and there is little party unity in the legislature, policy-making tends to be influenced primarily by an alliance of dominant groups (Vermont and Alabama are ex-

---

[7] Ibid., pp. 117-28.

amples). The presence of two-party competition and moderate legislative unity in the rural, nonindustrial states is associated with policy control by a single dominant interest (the influence of the Anaconda corporation in Montana or of Dupont in Delaware are examples). In more industrialized states with two-party competition and partisan unity in the legislature, we frequently encounter conflict over policy control between two major groups (Michigan, with conflict between automotive manufacturers and unions, is typical of this pattern). Finally, in urban states where parties are relatively weak (as in California), many interests have access to and partial control over the policy-making process.

The designation of such patterns of interest-group activity is helpful to the extent that it aids us in viewing the similarities of pressure politics in Texas and other states. Unfortunately, however, Texas does not fit conveniently into any one of the four categories. The past dominance of the oil industry in Texas, combined with a Democratic monopoly in statewide elections and the presence of poverty in the midst of affluence, leads many observers to classify Texas as dominated by a single major interest. Yet, given the marked urbanization and industrialization of Texas in the 1960s, the challenge of the Republican party, and the in-fighting between several interests in recent legislative sessions, one is tempted to view the Texas pressure system as undergoing a transformation from an alliance of dominant groups comprising an Establishment into a loose coalition of several major interests. To reach a judgment on this matter, we must first examine the variety of organized and unorganized interests in Texas.

## POLITICAL INTERESTS IN TEXAS

Few myths about Texas politics have endured as long as those that deal with the existence of an alleged Texas Establishment. The Establishment, so goes the tale, consists of a set of like-minded men, members of or allied with the major business interests in Texas, who control the state's economy, state and local governments, the educational system, news media, and other significant institutions to their own pecuniary advantage and to the detriment of the general population, particularly minority groups. This Establishment, says the argument, articulates and presses political demands in its interest while ignoring the problems and plights of the young, the poor whites, blacks, and Mexican-Americans. The bases of political support in Texas—ideological factions, the dominant Democratic party, the election system, and the general political culture—reinforce Establishment control of the political system as well as the system itself. Finally, the theory of the Establishment holds there is no viable alternative to the oligarchical rule of the Establishment, with the possible exception of the internally-torn Liberal faction of the Democratic party.[8]

Underlying the Establishment myth are assumptions about the nature of pressure politics, not only in Texas but elsewhere. One such assumption is that the unique advantage of a pressure group lies in its concentrating into one organization only those persons pursuing a common goal. The membership of a typical pressure organization, then, is relatively small compared to the general population of the state. Since the interest of the group is narrow and often exclusive, recruitment of members is selective. To broaden the base of membership would involve attracting persons who do not always share the same goals with the same intensities as do the group leaders. By concentrating a relatively small number of like-minded men in a pressure group, thus avoiding the danger of compromising goals in an appeal to a broader membership, group leaders more effectively mobilize resources for pressing political demands in conflict with other groups. In this sense the pressure system "is skewed, loaded and unbalanced in favor of a fraction of a minority" (an affluent class with resources to spend), a system which "probably 90 percent of the people cannot get into," and "not remarkably successful in mobilizing general interests" or even concerned with doing so.[9]

Paralleling this assumption that organized pressure groups press the demands of relatively few is another assumption about who the "relatively few" are and what type of politics they play. Business groups, it is held, have probably been the most active pressure groups in state politics for at least the last century. Over that period, so goes the assumption, they have solidified their influence in policy-making and assured themselves preferred treatment from a number of state legislatures, including that of Texas. Since the arrangement between these organized interests and public officials is congenial to both, the groups demand little in the way of new legislation or constitutional innovations. Rather, their interests lie in protecting what they already have, by preserving the status quo and insuring that whatever changes do occur inflict minimum harm to those interests. Their demands come not in the form of proposals for change, but as vetoes withholding support from proposals they regard as inimical to their interests. And, to assure that other groups will not press for threatening changes, vested interests agree not to support proposals which their allies deem disturbing. The result is a series of organizations, each exercising a veto over proposals under its narrow jurisdiction. Protection of privilege replaces leadership for change, and the followers "are those unorganized and sometimes dis-

---

[8] David Nevin, *The Texans* (New York: William Morrow & Co., Inc., 1968), pp. 183-84, 191-96.

[9] E. E. Schattschneider, *The Semisovereign People* (New York: Holt, Rinehart and Winston, 1960), pp. 34-35.

organized unfortunates who have not yet invented their group."[10] The result in Texas is a politics of "defer-and-demand"[11] as veto groups defer to one another and demand protection. In weighing the accuracy of these assumptions as they pertain to the Texas pressure system, we turn first to the interests represented in the so-called Establishment, then to those interests not represented at all.

## The Politics of Privilege

For Texas, as for all states, it is difficult to estimate the scope of the pressure system. Certainly, the number of interest organizations is sizable. For example, in 1967 there were more than 500 privately supported civic, commercial, and other nonprofit organizations in Texas engaged in statewide activities.[12] These included such politically involved groups as the American Legion, the Texas Apartment Association, the Texas State Building and Construction Trade Council, the Wholesale Beer Distributors of Texas, and the Texas League of Women Voters. Another indicator of the scale of pressure activity in Texas is the number of registered lobbyists in the state. In 1967 alone, 1996 lobbyists registered on behalf of pressure groups (the average number of lobbyists per legislative session in states keeping such records is approximately 275). On the other hand, we learn little about the importance of pressure-group activity in Texas from the amount of expenditures each group makes on lobbying activities. In 1967, the Texas Brewers Institute reported spending $6871 on lobbying, the oil and gas industry $12,342, and the Texas State Teachers' Association $2089.[13] Such small amounts conceal the fact that much of the money spent on pressure activity is directed toward electing sympathetic officials, thus minimizing the amount spent on influencing them, or simply not reported at all.

Our interest in the pressure politics of Texas, however, is not primarily in estimating the scale of interest-group activity, but rather its patterns at state and local levels, particularly the extent to which those patterns reflect the alliance of several dominant groups designated as the Establishment. Proponents of the Establishment theory argue that the dominant groups represent monied interests: "Money is power and power is money. The two go together, and in Texas it is almost impossible to have one without the

---

[10]David Riesman et al., *The Lonely Crowd* (Garden City, N. Y.: Doubleday & Co., 1955), p. 247.

[11]Lee Clark, "May the Lobby Hold You in the Palm of Its Hand," *The Texas Observer*, LX, May 24, 1968, p. 1.

[12]For a listing of these organizations, see the *Texas Almanac, 1968-69* (Dallas: The Dallas Morning News, 1968), pp. 507-21.

[13]The League of Women Voters of Texas, *The Texas Legislature* (Houston: League of Women Voters of Texas, 1967).

other."[14] Although there is insufficient evidence available to permit us to test this proposition in a meaningful way, any enumeration of the most influential Texas interests would include the oil industry, the beer industry, the railroads, the construction industry, natural gas businesses, insurance companies, the truckers, consumer finance agencies, and the banking industry. And we would need to include such satellite interests as the Farm Bureau, and the engineering lobby, and groups with certain economic concerns, such as religious bodies.

Yet, a listing of important economic interests actively engaged in politics does not prove either that the pressure system is the exclusive prerogative of an interlocking economic elite or that an Establishment unites behind a single set of goals. Other pressure organizations have access to governing officials. At the opening of the 1969 legislative session, for example, 115 of the 377 lobbyists registered with the Texas Legislature represented the Texas State Teachers' Association (a 125,000-member organization). Similarly, the A.F.L.-C.I.O. has long been active in electoral politics in Texas, and labor unions had 38 registered lobbyists in 1969. Furthermore, established economic interests frequently disagree on how to protect their vested positions. In the 1969 session of the Texas Legislature, for instance, proposals for raising needed revenues extended to increasing a tax on corporate franchises. In response, a number of corporate interests insisted instead upon a sales tax to be levied on restaurant patrons, beer sales, and entertainment. The alliance of established interests quickly split among themselves, with none winning absolute victory, and the final sales tax was a compromise "dictated" as much by efforts to reconcile differences between established interests as by the successful efforts of the Establishment to promote a single self-interest.

There is evidence that at local levels in Texas, alliances of established interests tend to be more unified. A study of the power structure in Dallas, conducted in 1961, reported the occupations of 64 persons ranked as "the most influential men in Dallas." Of these men, 41.8 percent were in commerce (real estate, trade, utilities, and communications), 31.3 percent were in the fields of finance (banking and insurance), 16.4 percent were in manufacturing, and the remainder were in law, and government. The study designated seven of these men as the "Key Leaders"—those involved in making the most significant community decisions; of the seven, three were bankers, two were utility executives, one was in the retail trade, and one was in industry.[15] To the extent that such localized power structures exist, they control

---

[14]Nevin, *The Texans*, p. 193.
[15]Carol Estes Thometz, *The Decision-Makers: The Power Structure of Dallas* (Dallas: Southern Methodist University Press, 1963), pp. 30-31.

policy-making in their own communities; but if community elites represent separate parochial interests within a broader statewide Establishment, the potential exists for inter-elite conflict, thus diminishing the chances for unified Establishment politics.

In addition, there are historical cleavages within the Texas Establishment that make elite cooperation in state and local politics even more difficult. Existing along with an older Texas aristocracy based upon land and cattle is an aristocracy of the nouveau riche, whose wealth, usually acquired in the last one or two generations, comes from business, finance, and industry. Although staunchly protective of its interests, the latter group is less oriented to the status quo, more receptive to marginal changes in established policies, and more pragmatic in political outlook. The differences in the economic orientations of the old and new aristocracies, combined with the growing difficulty of protecting all established interests and in pleasing all veto groups in an increasingly complex Texas social system, result in an underlying tension in the Texas Establishment. That tension frequently surfaces in the inability to find new sources of revenues, agree upon a unified system of higher education for the state, or compromise upon desirable candidates for public office. In instances of establishment feuds in electoral politics, at least, both Republicans and liberal Democrats in Texas have benefited from the split in forces.

To summarize, we can say that the pressure system in Texas represents primarily the interests of a loose alliance of the more affluent economic groups. These include not only economic groups peculiar to Texas, but also out-of-state interests such as national firms doing business within the state and thus having stakes in the outcome of policy struggles. Both the in-state and out-of-state groups are major economic interests acting as dominant articulators and suppliers of demands on the political system. These demands are more frequently exhibited as efforts to protect accrued privileges rather than extend them—the essence of veto politics. Bear in mind, however, that there are historical and economic divisions within the dominant alliance; moreover, the pressure system also provides access to policymakers for interests lying outside the economic oligarchy. As a result, the label "Establishment" refers not so much to a ruling clique of tightly interlocked interests as to a shifting coalition of privileged groups. If, therefore, an Establishment controls policy-making in Texas, it does so in the sense that its own internal conflicts over how to protect its separate interests define the concerns of Texas politicians. Thus, being preoccupied with resolving the internal struggles of a loosely coalesced Establishment, Texas officials may ignore and fail to represent the interests of the less affluent. It is this failure to represent and respond to the unorganized interests in Texas rather than any direct effort to rule them that lends credibility to the myth of the omnipotence of a Texas Establishment.

## The Ignored and Forgotten in Texas

If democratic rather than oligarchical control of the pressure system is to prevail in state government, then group politics must be open and competitive. With numerous groups competing against one another, the chances of successful domination by any single group or alliance of groups is reduced: "Organization for political action will produce counter-organization and, if the resources in the struggle approach equality, stalemate or compromise rather than total dominance may result."[16]

In Texas, however, the pressure system represents the demands of a loosely knit alliance of economic influentials because of the marked unevenness in the distribution of resources for political action. There are costs to organization, and not all elements in Texas are equally able to pay those costs. The result is that the unrepresented interests in Texas are primarily those whose poverty renders them incapable of large-scale organization. Thus, the ignored and forgotten in Texas are the impoverished whites, blacks, and Mexican-Americans.

That poverty exists in Texas is easily documented. Accepting the United States Census Bureau's definition of poverty as a family income of less than $3000 per year, 28.8 percent of Texas families were living in poverty in 1959 (the median family income in Texas that year was $4884). The nationwide proportion of families living in poverty in 1959 was 21.4 percent, which means that while approximately one in 20 American families lived in Texas, one of every 14 *poor* families in the United States resided in Texas.[17]

The extent of poverty varies from one subgroup of the Texas population to another. As Table 4-2 indicates, the incidence of poverty is higher among families of black and Mexican-American Texans than among families of whites. The presence of poverty among blacks and Mexican-Americans in Texas is 2.7 and 2.4 times higher, respectively, than among whites. For still other indicators that poverty is especially acute among Texas minorities, in 1960 four out of every 10 black families lived under conditions of extreme poverty (a family income of less than $2000 per year), and while

---

[16]Zeigler, "Interest Groups in the States," p. 112.

[17]Data on the distribution of poverty in Texas are taken from the following: William P. Kuvlesky et al., *Poverty in Texas* (College Station, Texas: Texas A. & M. University, Texas Agricultural Experiment Station, 1965); W. Kennedy Upham and Michael F. Lever, *Differentials in the Incidence of Poverty in Texas* (College Station, Texas: Texas A. & M. University, Texas Agricultural Experiment Station, 1966); Michael F. Lever and W. Kennedy Upham, *Poverty Among Nonwhite Families in Texas and the Nation* (College Station, Texas: Texas A. & M. University, Texas Agricultural Experiment Station, 1968): W. Kennedy Upham and David E. Wright, *Poverty Among Spanish Americans in Texas* (College Station, Texas: Texas A. & M. University, Texas Agricultural Experiment Station, 1966).

TABLE 4-2   Number and Proportion of Poverty-Level Families among Whites, Blacks, and Mexican-Americans in Texas and the United States, 1960

|  | All Families |  | Whites |  | Blacks |  | Mexican-American |  |
|---|---|---|---|---|---|---|---|---|
|  | No. | % | No. | % | No. | % | No. | % |
| United States | 9,626,454 | 21.4 | 7,327,113 | 16.4 | 2,035,223 | 47.8 | 242,903 | 34.8* |
| Texas | 687,965 | 28.8 | 395,598 | 21.3 | 152,704 | 57.7 | 139,663 | 51.6* |

Source: *U. S. Census of Population: 1960, Volume I, Part 45, Texas, Tables 86 and 99; U. S. Census of Population: 1960, Subject Reports, Persons of Spanish Surname, Final Report PC (2)-1B, Table 5; U. S. Census of Population: 1960, Volume I, Part 1—United States Summary, Table 227.*
Note: Poverty is defined as a family income of less than $3000 per year.

*Limited to persons with Spanish surnames in five states—Texas, Arizona, California, Colorado, and New Mexico.

only 11 percent of the families in Texas in 1960 had Spanish surnames, 20 percent of the low-income families in Texas that year were Mexican-American. Interestingly enough, for all subgroups—white, black, and Mexican-American—the rate of poverty is higher in Texas than in the United States as a whole.[18]

Poverty makes it difficult to press political demands. And indeed, if some elements of the Texas population are disproportionately impoverished, it is unlikely that they are represented in policy-making at all. Such disproportion clearly exists in Texas and is dependent, as we shall see, not only on whether an individual is black or Mexican-American, but also on his place of residence, occupation, employment status, age, sex, education, and family type.

*Residence Differentials.* The degree of poverty in Texas varies significantly from one region to another. In the 1960s, one-half or more of the families residing in one-fourth of the Texas counties were poor. The counties with high rates of poverty were concentrated in the regions of South Texas and East Texas. The Mexican-American population is heavily concentrated in South Texas, and in 70 percent of the counties in this general region more than half the Mexican-American families were poor. The U.S.

---

[18]U. S. census data on Texas subgroups are classified according to whites, nonwhites, and persons with Spanish surnames. Reference to Mexican-Americans in the text is to persons included in the U. S. Census Bureau's Spanish Surname category, reference to blacks is to persons included in the Census Bureau's nonwhite category, and reference to whites is to those classified as whites by the Census Bureau, minus persons with Spanish surnames.

Census Bureau classified six of the counties in South Texas—Starr, Zapata, Zavala, Jim Hogg, Maverick, and Dimmit—as among the 300 poorest counties in the nation. East Texas is a region of high poverty levels for black Texans. Of 90 counties in that region, all but six had half or more of their black families living in poverty; in 34 counties, 80 percent or more of the black families were impoverished. Among other concentrations of poverty were the areas around the Big Bend and the Red River, which together accounted for one percent of the state's impoverished.

Poverty in Texas is nearly twice as prevalent in rural areas as in urban ones. Eighty-six percent of all Texas counties (accounting for 80 percent of the Texas population) had a higher rate of poverty among rural than among urban families. Yet, while a large number of poor families reside in rural areas, bear in mind that the majority of Texas poor are urban dwellers; thus, although a larger proportion of rural Texans are poor, most of the impoverished families in Texas are concentrated in urban areas. Looking at rural-urban differences in terms of ethnic minorities, relatively more of the white than the black impoverished live in rural areas; by the same token, relatively more of the black than white impoverished live in urban areas. Slightly under three-fourths of the state's Mexican-Americans living in poverty dwell in urban areas.

*Occupational Differences.* Occupations generally regarded in America as unskilled—service work, household work, manual labor, etc.—are also low-income occupations, so that we can expect the incidence of poverty to be higher for the unskilled than the skilled. Two out of every three heads of white families in 1960 in Texas were in a skilled occupation, but only one in five heads of black families was so employed. This alone might be expected to account for the much higher incidence of poverty among black than white Texans. Yet even when we compare whites and blacks in the same category, skilled or unskilled, the incidence of poverty among blacks exceeds that of whites. For example, 5 percent of white Texans in professional and technical occupations earned a family income below the poverty level, but almost 20 percent of professionally and technically employed blacks were poor. Similarly, 40 percent of black craftsmen were poor, but only 13 percent of white craftsmen. In unskilled categories, the levels of black and white poverty appeared to be slightly more equal; for instance, of black laborers not on the farm, half existed in poverty, and of whites in similar occupations, 42 percent did. In summary, the differences in rates of black and white poverty in Texas cannot be attributed solely to occupational factors, since the much higher incidence of poverty among blacks holds across skilled and unskilled categories.

Of course, many Texans have no occupations at all; that is, they are unemployed. At the close of the 1960s, for example, between 3 and 4 percent of Texans (excluding the young, students, housewives, retired workers, seasonal workers in an "off" season and not looking for work, the institutionalized, mentally ill, and disabled) were unemployed. Obviously, the more frequently or longer a person is unemployed, the more likely he is to earn less for his family than the $3000 poverty-level income. Interestingly enough, in the period of the 1960 census, black families in Texas had proportionately more of their members employed than did white families. Yet, low incomes were common among wage-earning blacks, whether the employment was steady or interrupted because of illness, hiring and firing, or whatever. For Mexican-Americans, unemployment was relatively high; 8 percent were unemployed at the close of the 1960s, compared to 3 percent of the whites.

*Educational Disparities.* In Texas, as in the nation generally, the lower a person's educational level, the higher his rate of poverty. In 1960 only 6 percent of families headed by college graduates were impoverished, compared with 40 percent in which the head had only an elementary school education (8 years or less). Both black and Mexican-Americans in Texas have considerably less education than whites. The median years of school completed in 1960 by persons over 25 years of age was 6.1 for Mexican-Americans, 8.1 for blacks, and 11.5 for whites. But members of minorities at each level of education had a much higher rate of poverty than did members of the white majority. Thus, as with occupation and employment, poverty among minority groups is relatively higher even when the educational level is held constant.

*Age and Sex Differences.* Families in Texas with either very young or very old heads tend to have higher rates of poverty than those whose heads are in intermediate age categories. For example, 60 percent of the families headed by persons over 65 lived in poverty in 1960, as did 40 percent of those headed by persons under 25. This generalization holds for our three subgroups of impoverished—white, black, and Mexican-American—but, again, the impoverishment is greater with the minorities.

Poverty among families with female heads is very common in Texas; in 1959 over 60 percent of the families headed by females lived in poverty, compared to 25 percent of the families headed by males. Once more, the incidence of poverty among minorities exceeds that of whites. For example, 82 percent of the black families headed by females had an income of less than $3000 in 1959.

The comparatively substantial presence in Texas of families headed by the very young or old and of families where the mother or father is missing because of death, divorce, separation, or desertion suggests another factor related to poverty in the state. Broken families or those with aged or very young heads are frequently poverty-stricken. In Texas, 50 percent of the white families and 80 percent of the black families with aged or lone heads are poor; moreover, the rate of poverty among these blacks is higher than among such blacks in the nation as a whole, and, as might be expected, considerably higher than among the Texas whites.

We can summarize this discussion of the correlates of Texas poverty by saying that poverty is disproportionately high among minorities, rural residents, the unskilled, the unemployed, the uneducated, and among families with heads not likely to be employed—the very young, the aged, and women. The most significant disparity, however, is between the white majority and the black and Mexican-American minorities. Regardless of age, sex, residence, occupation, education, or employment, the incidence of poverty is markedly higher for minorities than whites. This suggests that other factors than those reviewed contribute to the disproportionately high levels of poverty among minorities. As one study suggests, "A likely candidate may be discrimination or prejudicial practices which prevent nonwhites in Texas from attaining income levels available to Texas whites or U.S. nonwhites with comparable levels of education and skill. While such a proposition may be unpalatable, ignoring the possibility that it may be accurate is foolish and even dangerous."[19]

At best we have only fragmentary data pertaining to the degree and impact of discrimination against minorities in Texas. Table 4-3 summarizes the findings of annual statewide surveys of the acceptance by Texas whites of integration in the 1960s. The average proportion of whites accepting integration measures was 32 percent in 1963, 42 percent in 1964, 44 percent in 1966, 56 percent in 1968, and 55 percent—a negligible decline—in 1969. It is interesting, however, that despite the steady rise in acceptance, almost one-fourth of Texas whites still do not wish to *work* side by side with blacks. And, turning to other evidence, it is noteworthy that even in some of the political subsystems of Texas, fewer blacks are employed in governmental positions than their relative numbers in the local population would lead us to expect. For example, blacks in 1965 comprised 23 percent of Houston's population but only 19 percent of its employees; and blacks constituted 20 percent of the Harris County population in 1960, yet made up less than 6 percent of the county's employed as late as 1967.[20]

Regardless of the extent to which discriminatory attitudes may contribute to minority poverty in Texas, the fact remains that in the 1960s almost 30 percent of all Texas families hardly possessed the resources for an adequate standard of living, let alone for organized and effective political activity. It is doubtful that the situation has changed much since then. Given the opportunity to participate in the anti-poverty programs developed

---

[19]Lever and Upham, *Poverty Among Nonwhite Families*, p. 75.

[20]United States Commission on Civil Rights, *For All the People . . . By All the People: A Report on Equal Opportunity in State and Local Government Employment* (Washington, D.C.: U. S. Government Printing Office, 1969), p. 6.

TABLE 4-3  Attitudes of Texas Whites Toward Racial Integration, 1963-1969

| Form of Integration:<br>Would you accept: | 1963 | 1964 | 1966 | 1968 | 1969 |
|---|---|---|---|---|---|
| **Negroes riding in the same sections of trains and buses with you?** | | | | | |
| Accept | 49% | 62% | 64% | 80% | 75% |
| Reject | 47 | 35 | 35 | 19 | 23 |
| No Answer | 4 | 3 | 1 | 1 | 2 |
| **Negroes eating in the same restaurant with you?** | | | | | |
| Accept | 40 | 54 | 56 | 73 | 71 |
| Reject | 57 | 44 | 42 | 26 | 28 |
| No Answer | 3 | 2 | 2 | 1 | 1 |
| **Negroes staying in the same hotel with you?** | | | | | |
| Accept | 36 | 49 | 50 | 66 | 64 |
| Reject | 60 | 47 | 48 | 32 | 34 |
| No Answer | 4 | 4 | 2 | 2 | 2 |
| **Sending your children to the same schools?** | | | | | |
| Accept | 41 | 52 | 53 | 69 | 65 |
| Reject | 55 | 46 | 45 | 29 | 32 |
| No Answer | 4 | 2 | 2 | 2 | 3 |
| **Negroes attending your church?** | | | | | |
| Accept | 46 | 59 | 54 | 68 | 68 |
| Reject | 50 | 38 | 43 | 30 | 31 |
| No Answer | 4 | 3 | 3 | 2 | 1 |
| **Negroes using the same swimming pool with you?** | | | | | |
| Accept | 19 | 27 | 29 | 35 | 39 |
| Reject | 77 | 69 | 68 | 60 | 58 |
| No Answer | 4 | 4 | 3 | 5 | 3 |
| **Negroes working side by side with you in the same kind of job?** | | | | | |
| Accept | 56 | 67 | 69 | 83 | 76 |
| Reject | 40 | 31 | 29 | 16 | 22 |
| No Answer | 4 | 2 | 2 | 1 | 2 |
| **Negroes attending the same social gathering outside your home?** | | | | | |
| Accept | 23 | 32 | 37 | 49 | 48 |
| Reject | 73 | 65 | 61 | 48 | 50 |
| No Answer | 4 | 3 | 2 | 3 | 2 |
| **Negroes attending a social gathering in your home?** | | | | | |
| Accept | 13 | 19 | 23 | 31 | 33 |
| Reject | 83 | 77 | 75 | 67 | 64 |
| No Answer | 4 | 4 | 2 | 2 | 3 |

## TABLE 4-3 (Continued)

| Form of Integration: Would you accept: | 1963 | 1964 | 1966 | 1968 | 1969 |
|---|---|---|---|---|---|
| Negroes living next door to you? | | | | | |
| Accept | 23 | 30 | 29 | 38 | 41 |
| Reject | 74 | 67 | 69 | 59 | 56 |
| No Answer | 3 | 3 | 2 | 3 | 3 |
| Having a Negro as roommate for your son or daughter at college? | | | | | |
| Accept | 8 | 14 | 18 | 21 | 24 |
| Reject | 88 | 82 | 80 | 74 | 71 |
| No Answer | 4 | 4 | 2 | 5 | 5 |

*Source: "The Texas Poll," The Dallas Morning News, September 14, 1969.*

under the Economic Opportunity Act, Texas spent $17.77 per person on such programs, the eighth lowest expenditure of any state in the nation, placing the Texas anti-poverty effort at the level of such economically underdeveloped states as Kansas, South Carolina, Alabama, and Louisiana.[21]

To conclude this section on interest groups, three distinctive sets of interests exist in Texas politics. First, there is the loosely knit alliance of economic affluents whose demands are disproportionately represented in policy-making through the pressure system. Second, there are the impoverished, who may have a few organizations (such as labor unions or teachers' associations) representing them in pressure politics, but who in general are without the resources conducive either to voicing political demands or lending political support. Finally, there are numerous interests that are neither affluent nor impoverished—a pluralist grouping of middle-income Texans with both unified and conflicting goals, with access to the pressure system, who support the established constitutional regime, institutions, and policies resulting from the interplay of established interests. Thus, pressure politics in Texas is the politics of the "haves" rather than the "have nots." Going now to the "haves," what are the techniques and what is the effectiveness of established pressure groups?

## TECHNIQUES OF DEMAND POLITICS

To have their demands satisfied, pressure groups must first obtain access to the key offices where policy decisions are made.[22] The word "access"

---

[21] Andrew T. Cowart, "Anti-Poverty Expenditures in the American States: A Comparative Analysis," *Midwest Journal of Political Science*, XIII (May 1969), 226.
[22] Truman, *The Governmental Process*, pp. 264-70.

here implies identifying key officials, having contact with them, influencing them. There are several techniques pressure groups use in state politics to promote effective access. Among the most important are those guaranteeing privileged contact with decision-makers, campaigns on behalf of political candidates and policies, lobbying, and demonstrative behavior.

## INSTITUTIONALIZING PRIVILEGE

The effectiveness of organized interests is determined in part by the ways the structure of state government facilitates or restricts group contact with officials. In states where administrators are directly responsible to the Governor, pressures upon a particular policy-maker succeed to the extent that the governor acquiesces to decisions made by that official. Even when administrators are directly responsible to the Governor, they may retain considerable discretion to act independently and thus respond to pressure from interests to which the Governor himself may not by sympathetic. However, if they are isolated from gubernatorial or legislative control, pressure-group influence over them stands an even greater chance of success. It stands to reason, then, that pressure groups are vitally concerned with any constitutional or legislative arrangements that define or modify official control over various offices.

A recent study explored the extent to which interest-group strength in the states correlated with constitutional provisions determining the degree of gubernatorial or legislative control over administrative agencies. (The preferred method for isolating agencies from such control is to have agency officials elected; if agency officials are appointed by the Governor, they are responsible to him and dominated less often by state pressure groups.) As we might expect, the study revealed that the stronger the interest groups, the greater the number of elected state officials, the greater the number of state agencies with elected officials, the greater the likelihood that state public utility commissions (agencies regulating rates charged by various business interests) are elected, and the greater the probability that judges on state courts of last resort are elected.[23]

Organized interests also institutionalize their privileges by obtaining favorable policy decisions and then preventing regular legislative review of those decisions by securing constitutional amendments protecting them. Many states have long constitutions, specific in detail, insulating certain activities from legislative "meddling." The comparative study of state constitutions and interest groups referred to above revealed that the stronger the interest groups, the greater the length of state constitutions, the greater

---

[23]Lewis A. Froman, Jr., "Some Effects of Interest Group Strength in State Politics," *American Political Science Review*, LX (December 1966), 952-62.

the number of proposed amendments, the greater the number of amendments adopted, and the less the difficulty of amending the constitution.[24]

Each of the factors providing special access for organized interests—lengthy constitutions, numerous specific amendments, and an abundance of semi-autonomous administrative agencies—is typical of the Texas political system. Certainly the Texas Constitution is lengthy (over 50,000 words in the 1960s and more than three times the median length of all state constitutions); certainly it is an oft-amended document (almost 200 amendments in less than a century—again, three times the average of other state constitutions—and with only three of the original seventeen articles still unchanged);[25] and certainly the "perfect" constitution of 1876 (now "perfected" even more by 200 changes) is detailed and complex, even to the point, for instance, of describing penalties for any person engaging in a duel, including the gentleman acting as a second.

Established privilege is most effectively protected in Texas, however, through the creation of isolated and independent bureaus, boards, and commissions responsive to the demands of vested interests. Indeed, so many such agencies have been provided by constitutional amendment, or by the legislature fulfilling the dictates of an amendment, that no accurate accounting of the total number even exists (estimates range from 150 to 250).[26] The vast majority of agencies perform routine duties (licensing, reviewing election results, leasing land, etc.), but the remainder—for example, the State Board of Education, the Highway Commission, and the Railroad Commission—make far-reaching policy decisions. Whatever the number and functions, in all but a few cases the agencies responsible for making and applying policy affecting major state interests are headed by part-time boards and commissions who pay relatively little attention to relations between the agency and its interest-group clientele. However, the critical operations of each agency (at least from the perspective of pressure groups) are actually in the hands of an executive director who, while usually chosen by the part-time board or commission members, often retains his position by winning the respect and goodwill of the interests his agency purportedly regulates. He gains this interest support by responding to interest demands and appointing lesser agency officials friendly to, and perhaps even suggested by, the agency clientele.

The heads of state agencies (whether individuals, boards, or commissions) are elected, serve ex officio, or, most commonly, are gubernatorial appointees. Although gubernatorial appointment usually means guberna-

---

[24]*Ibid.*, p. 961.

[25]Dick Smith, "Constitutional Revision: Attempts to Unshackle Texas," *Comment*, XV (November 1969), 2.

[26]*Texas Almanac*, pp. 615-23.

torial control, this is not the case in Texas. The Texas Constitution substantially restricts appointive power as a method of exerting control over agencies by requiring Senatorial confirmation, demanding specific qualifications for the type of person who may be appointed, and staggering the length of terms of agency heads. Each of these restrictions strengthens the likelihood of pressure-group influence. Senatorial confirmation makes it necessary for a Governor to appoint agency heads acceptable to individual Senators in order to prevent a Senator from exercising his privilege under senatorial courtesy of asking his colleagues to repudiate what he regards as an offensive appointment. Since major organized interests have effective access to state Senators, this often means that pressure groups, in effect, veto an undesirable appointment. The requirement that specific qualifications be met for appointment—for instance, that a board member come from a particular region or be in a particular occupation—forces a Governor to choose an agency head from the very interest the agency is designed to regulate. Finally, the staggering of the length of terms of agency heads limits control over the agencies themselves. For example, an agency may be headed by a six-member board, each member serving a six-year term, but with only one-third of that membership appointed every two years. Since a Governor serves only a two-year term (and seldom is re-elected more than once), he is not in office long enough to appoint all members of the board and may actually have the opportunity to appoint but a minority of the board's membership.

In sum, the Texas Constitution, because of its detailed provisions affecting major policy areas and its tendency to isolate key decision-makers from formal gubernatorial control, both facilitates the access of established pressure groups to policy-makers and acts as an effective shield for protecting their privileges against the scrutiny of reform-minded elective officials.

## CAMPAIGNING FOR CANDIDATES AND POLICIES

Organized interests promote their influence over policy-making by committing their resources to two types of campaigns—the election of public officials and the promotion of specific policy measures. The purpose of electoral activity by pressure groups is obvious—to place in office candidates responsive to interest demands. With these candidates in office, future access to them is assured. Or more succinctly, "the game is over before the legislature meets."[27]

The principal contribution of an organized interest to a sympathetic candidate is to assume a share of his campaign costs. Granted, the Texas

---

[27]The League of Women Voters of Texas, *The Texas Legislature*, p. 2.

Election Code endeavors to regulate campaign expenditures and contributions: candidates must make itemized reports of expenses, debts incurred, and gifts; any contributor of more than $100 must report his gift if the candidate does not; corporations and labor unions may not contribute; and contributions are not tax-deductible. But these regulations border on the meaningless. No ceiling is placed on either expenditures or contributions; a gubernatorial campaign easily costs $500,000, and legislative races sometimes involve $50,000. Nor can regulations check the ingenious subterfuges that evade prohibitions on corporate and union financing. Among these are the provision of the candidate's staff (the contributor pays their salaries as a legitimate business expense, yet never has them work as part of his own business staff), free office space, travel in company cars or planes, printing, envelopes, stationery, and even postage stamps. Labor unions employ another technique—fund-raising drives among their members, thus meeting the letter of the law by contributing individual, not union, donations.

Modern election campaigns, particularly for important offices in Texas, are professionally managed contests involving the expertise of public relations personnel, opinion pollsters, and mass media experts. In Texas, major businesses and corporations employ public relations firms on a regular basis; these firms include the Read-Poland agency, the Rominger agency, the Hyde agency, Malec-Ready, Collin-Knaffs, Kaplan-Chamberlain, and Rives, Dyke and Company. In election years they work for statewide and local candidates, preparing speeches, arranging advertising, mobilizing volunteers, etc. Their fees, of course, can be paid by the interested business firm, which "loans" the candidate their services. And corporations frequently hire polling firms to survey a candidate's chances and assess his image, but mask the poll by adding "trailer" questions about a new product on which they want consumer reaction; moreover, since the poll does serve a minor business purpose, a corporation can write off the cost as a tax-deductible expense.

The electoral efforts of pressure groups extend beyond financial contributions. Some groups bless a candidacy through public endorsement or crucify it through public disapproval. Liberals in Texas actively seek AFL-CIO endorsement, since it may draw money from labor interests outside the state. Not all endorsements are public; major interests "pass the word" to allied groups about a candidate who has agreed to support them in the legislature. Finally, we should not omit the active effort of pressure groups between elections that contributes to later electoral outcomes. Groups finance and conduct voter registration drives to politicize previously indifferent interests; one such group, for example, is the Political Association of Spanish-speaking Organizations.

However, not all political campaigning by pressure groups is directed toward electing legislative lackeys. Sometimes a bill facing the state legislature involves established interests. Groups mobilize public sentiment for or against the measure, or at least build the illusion that the public has taken such a stand and that legislators should heed it. Interested parties retain public relations firms, buy advertising in newspapers and on television, and instigate letter-writing campaigns designed to deluge legislators with telegrams, postal cards, and letters voicing group positions. Although the "ground swell of public opinion" is anything but spontaneous, the magnitude of the outpouring of these instigated communications gives legislators cause for "second thoughts."

*LOBBYING FOR DEMANDS*

Perhaps the most frequently employed (and most publicized) technique of organized interests for pressing demands is lobbying. Because of its prevalence at all levels of government—national, state, and local—let us first examine the technique in comparative perspective before describing the tactics and effects of Texas lobbying.

## Lobbying in State Politics

Lobbying is an activity carried out by representatives of organized interests and directed toward influencing policy-makers on behalf of those interests. As a communication link between pressure groups and legislative officials, the lobbyist transmits group demands to policy-makers and official positions back to the group. Lobbyists and legislators both function as representative elites: the former are selected by established interests for the purpose of playing some role in policy-making, and the latter are elected to positions of policy-making authority. Although they do not represent geographically defined constituencies as do legislators, lobbyists still voice the views of large numbers of people in organized groups.[28]

Legislators and lobbyists are similar in other ways as well. For one thing, neither legislating nor lobbying is a full-time occupation at the state level. While serving in the legislature many legislators continue in the occupation they had prior to election, as lawyers, teachers, insurance agents, farmers, etc. Similarly, most state lobbyists engage in other activities than lobbying, spending perhaps only half their time on influencing votes in a legislative session. Also, in many respects the personal characteristics of lobbyists and legislators are similar. Both groups usually consist of whites, males, Protestants, the young to middle-aged, and the fairly well educated. Differences in median family income between the two groups are usually

---

[28]Harmon Zeigler and Michael Baer, *Lobbying: Interaction and Influence in American State Legislatures* (Belmont, Cal.: Wadsworth Publishing Co., 1969), p. 38.

small, and members of both tend to have professional or managerial backgrounds (often they are lawyers).[29]

For all the similarities between legislators and lobbyists, however, there are also interesting differences. Lobbying is a less permanent endeavor than office-holding. State lobbyists tend to move from job to job, traveling in and out of political employment. A study of legislator-lobbyist relations in four states—Massachusetts, North Carolina, Oregon, and Utah—reveals that legislators tend to be "self-starters"; that is, they are motivated to seek a political career on their own, often because of ideological inspiration or a calculated plan for success. Lobbyists, however, drift into their occupation without having made a deliberate choice; once in lobbying, their careers are varied as they continue to jump in and out of politics.[30] Results from a study of Oklahoma lobbying are typical: while most lobbyists had been engaged in lobbying in previous legislative sessions, a large number were newcomers.[31]

## Lobbying in Texas

There have been few studies of lobbying in Texas. What evidence we have, however, suggests that Texas lobbying is generally similar to that in other states, but with certain notable differences. We can estimate the number of lobbyists in Texas politics by examining lobby registration figures. Since 1957, all persons appearing before committees or making direct approaches to legislators in order to promote or oppose a bill have been required to register with the Chief Clerk of the House of Representatives. In addition, all persons spending as much as $50 for direct communication with members during sessions are required to file expense statements. Registration figures overstate the number of lobbyists in Austin, since not all persons testifying before committees are really paid lobbyists of organized interests; by the same token, however, estimates often understate the magnitude of Texas lobbying because the registration figures ignore between-session lobbying activity and because of the relative ease of evading registration whatsoever. Furthermore, many interests lobby directly through the legislator they helped elect rather than employ a lobbyist in Austin.

Since the 1957 act requiring registration of lobbyists, Texas has had a high of 4534 registered lobbyists (1959) and a low of 377 (1969). The num-

---

[29]Samuel C. Patterson, "The Role of the Lobbyist: The Case of Oklahoma," *Journal of Politics*, 25 (February 1963), 90; Malcolm E. Jewell and Samuel C. Patterson, *The Legislative Process in the United States* (New York: Random House, 1966), pp. 281-82; Harmon Zeigler and Michael A. Baer, "The Recruitment of Lobbyists and Legislators," *Midwest Journal of Political Science*, XII (August 1968), 497-500.

[30]Zeigler and Baer, "The Recruitment of Lobbyists and Legislators," p. 500.

[31]Patterson, "The Role of the Lobbyist," pp. 77-79.

ber of registered lobbyists declined throughout the 1960s, with 3153 in 1961, 2022 in 1965, and 1996 in 1967. Reported amounts spent on lobbying have also declined. As one would expect, registered lobbyists—both amateur and paid—tend to represent the established or moderately affluent interests in Texas. In 1969, for example, the Texas Manufacturer's Association registered 3 lobbyists; the oil and gas industries, 22; public utilities firms, 19; cities and chambers of commerce, 19; the insurance industry, 14; restaurants, 13; and the railroads, 10. Texas school teachers, lobbying in 1969 for pay increases, had 115 registered lobbyists; school boards and administrations, 8; and labor unions, 38. With proposals to legalize liquor sales by the drink in 1969, the beer industry registered 7 lobbyists and the liquor firms 3. In the same year, three of the Governor's advisors were registered lobbyists (all for private associations), and five former House members registered as lobbyists for private concerns. In general, the entrenched interests used fewer lobbyists in 1969 than normal, but not so few as would appear from the registration count; those registered included only professional, not part-time, agents.

Indeed, Texas lobbying is notably less the amateur or part-time endeavor that it is elsewhere. Instead of hiring individuals for lobbying merely during legislative sessions, the established interests maintain a professional lobbyist corps with permanent Austin offices (many own their own buildings). In the 1960s almost a thousand persons were employed by such interests to maintain contacts with state boards and commissions (principally with their executive directors) and with legislators.[32] In the face of such a commitment to lobbying on the part of the established interests, it is little wonder that interests which characteristically lack, or even avoid, participation in formal and voluntary organizations find it difficult to press demands; Mexican-Americans, who avoid organized politics, are a case in point.[33]

Neither numbers nor professionalization, however, guarantee access. There are, therefore, many tactics employed to facilitate contact and good will between lobbyists and officials. Aside from the normal devices (contributions to election campaigns, phone calls, telegrams, personal visits, the placing of legislators on payrolls of organized interests through "retainer" fees, etc.), Texas lobbyists promote interaction with policy-makers by ingenious techniques. If, for example, members of the legislature throw a party, lobbyists eagerly supply the necessary liquid refreshment. Similarly, lobbyists invite legislators out for breakfast, lunch, or dinner, and have even been known to pay legislators' apartment or hotel bills. One legislator's wife reports how the Representatives' Wives Club has become a forum where

---

[32]Allen Duckworth, "Lobbying in Texas," *The Dallas Morning News,* September 10-15, 1961.

[33]Arthur J. Rubel, *Across the Tracks: Mexican-Americans in a Texas City* (Austin: University of Texas Press, 1966), Chap. 6.

lobbyists purchase goodwill by buying dinners and gifts for the spouses of officials.[34] And during the Christmas season new legislators are invited to select gifts from brochures provided by lobbyists, the gifts to be supplied free of charge. Finally, there are two quaint customs, "Speaker's Day" and "Governor for a Day." The former, originally a day set aside for legislative members to bestow a gift on the House Speaker, later became an occasion for lobbyists to lavish their largess on legislators for past and future services rendered. Similarly, when a Senator acts as Governor (when the Governor and Lieutenant Governor are temporarily absent from the state), his friends —particularly his lobbyist friends—honor him with festivities and gifts. Although both Speaker's Day and Governor-for-a-Day are less profitable for the honorees than they once were, the traditions are reminders of the free and open interaction that is typical between lobbyists and legislators.

The legislator-lobbyist interaction, however, is not a one-way street. Granted, the lobbyist favors the legislator with lavish attention and money in order to gain legislative support for the passage or defeat of a measure. But to focus on what the lobbyist gets from the legislator ignores the fact that legislators also use lobbyists to enhance their own influence. Lobbyists perform a variety of services in the expectation that they will someday be rewarded. First, a legislator may enlist a lobbyist's help in influencing another legislator. In Oregon, for example, 55 percent of the lobbyists reported that they had been asked by legislators to perform such a service, and 53 percent of the legislators reported having made this request of lobbyists. We have no comparable figures for Texas, but we suspect that this form of mutual assistance takes place there as well. Second, legislators ask lobbyists to mobilize pressure groups on behalf of a specific measure. Again, we have no evidence of how frequently this occurs in Texas, but we know that both legislators and lobbyists report such requests in Massachusetts, North Carolina, Oregon, and Utah. Third, lobbyists frequently enter into the planning of strategy for how best to steer a bill through the legislature or how best to kill it. Such a legislator-lobbyist coalition is particularly influential when it comes to *defeating* legislation, the very essence of "veto group" activity. This is because any piece of legislation in order to win approval must overcome a series of obstacles—it must be assigned to a committee whose members are sympathetic with its aims, it must receive favorable committee action, it must be reported out of committee, it must be placed on the legislative calendar for debate, it must come to a vote, and it must receive a majority of favorable votes from legislators. If the legislator-lobbyist coalition can convince but one key legislative officer to oppose the bill in this process (say, for example, get the presiding officer to refer the bill to an unfavorable committee or get a committee chairman to oppose

---

[34]Clark, "May the Lobby Hold You in the Palm of its Hand," pp. 21-22.

the measure), legislative defeat for the proposal is largely assured.[35] Finally, legislators use lobbyists not only to extend their influence as policy-makers, but also to acquire information. That information includes both an assessment of the degree of public and legislative support for a measure and technical expertise on the various complexities of a bill. For the novice legislator (approximately one-third of Texas legislators in each session are new) with hardly any staff and little time for research, the technical guidance of an experienced lobbyist is of immeasurable assistance. For an aspiring politician it is a service ultimately of more value than a free lunch or Christmas gift and may well be longer remembered.

Students of lobbyist-legislator relations have suggested that lobbyists engage in different styles of lobbying, that is, that there are several basic techniques employed in performing the twin functions of persuading and informing legislators. The *contact man*, for example, exerts influence by visiting legislators or administrators, cultivating their friendship, discussing with them the complexities of legislative routine, and becoming an informal confidant. The *campaign organizer*, in contrast, solidifies his influence by assisting the legislator's election effort—contributing money, mobilizing support back home, etc. The *informant* builds his influence by providing data on proposals and programs; if he is competent, he becomes a recognized "expert" in specific policy areas and no legislator would think of acting in those areas without first checking the details with him. The *watchdog* performs his job by staying abreast of legislative developments, closely scrutinizing the legislative calendar, and snooping in the legislative corridors and administrative offices; thus, he can alert his interest group to pending measures and to unexpected attacks on privilege. Finally, the *strategist* works with legislators and other lobbyists in planning campaigns for specific proposals and for the election of sympathetic legislators; the strategist is often a public relations man who works on behalf of certain candidacies and then sells particular measures to the very legislators he helped elect.[36] We have no way of knowing what proportion of Texas lobbyists practice each of these styles. We would hypothesize, however, that contact men and campaign organizers are particularly common, that strategists are increasing their influence, and that both informants and watchdogs play a lesser role in Texas policy-making.

---

[35]Harmon Zeigler, "The Effects of Lobbying: A Comparative Assessment," *Western Political Quarterly*, XXII (March 1969), 122-40.
[36]Jewell and Patterson, *The Legislative Process*, pp. 285-89.

## Effects of Lobbying

Observers of the Texas lobby differ in their evaluation of the effectiveness of lobbyists on policy-making. Some, for example, suggest that the lobby may hold the state "in the palm of its hand."[37] Others attribute influence to the lobby, but see "something of a checks and balances angle—the truck lobbyists against the rails; the power companies against the rural co-ops, home builders against oil companies on city annexation laws."[38] Few observers, however, dismiss Texas lobbyists as without any influence. To the extent that Texas lobbyists do influence policy, several factors determine their overall impact. These include the perceptions of lobbyists and legislators, characteristics of the legislature, and attempts to regulate lobbying.

Just as lobbyists have identifiable styles in their relations with officials, so do legislators respond to lobbyists in different ways. A study of legislator-lobbyist relations in California, Tennessee, Ohio, and New Jersey suggests that there are three types of legislative response. Some legislators are *facilitators*, exhibiting a friendly attitude toward organized interests and a great deal of knowledge about group activity. Others are *resisters*, who also know a great deal about the activity of organized groups but are hostile to it. And, finally, there are the *neutrals*, who either have no strong feelings about group pressure (when they know of it) or have little knowledge of group activity regardless of their feelings.[39]

The evidence regarding the response of Texas legislators to pressure groups suggests that there are more neutrals than clear-cut facilitators or resisters. One researcher asked a sample of Texas lobbyists to rate each legislator on how favorable his voting behavior was to the particular lobbyist's organization. Lobbyists included represented the A.F.L.-C.I.O., bankers, conservative religious groups, the Farm Bureau, the Texas Manufacturers Association, the Texas Medical Association, the Texas Motor Transportation Association, the Texas Municipal League, and the Texas State Teachers Association. In most cases, the lobbyists rated their voting behavior "neither favorable nor unfavorable," but with more ratings leaning toward "favorable" or "very favorable" and none toward "unfavorable" or "very unfavorable."[40] It should be remembered, however, that these are lobbyists' perceptions, not legislators'; nor do such ratings indicate how lob-

---

[37]Clark, "May the Lobby Hold You in the Palm of its Hand," p. 3.
[38]Duckworth, "Lobbying in Texas."
[39]John C. Wahlke, Heinz Eulau, William Buchanan, and Leroy C. Ferguson, *The Legislative System* (New York: John Wiley and Sons, Inc., 1962), pp. 324-25.
[40]Jerry B. Michel and Sheila D. Sheinberg, "Rural-Urban Differences in a Southwestern State Legislature and Some Probable Consequences of Redistricting," paper presented at the Joint Meetings of the Southern Sociological Society and the Southwestern Sociological Association, New Orleans, Louisiana, April 1966.

byists might rate the legislators' activity in committee, where bills favorable or unfavorable to organized interests are hammered out.

The most significant characteristic of the Texas Legislature which facilitates lobbyist influence is the general quality of amateurism pervading the membership. As we have already pointed out, legislative duty is generally a part-time, not full-time, professional endeavor. Pay levels are too low to make legislative diligence rewarding. Legislative staffs are small, hardly sufficient to educate the inexperienced legislator with regard to either his role or specific issues. And the Texas legislator *is* basically inexperienced. A study covering fourteen terms of the House of Representatives (1935-1961) reveals that almost 40 percent of the members had no previous legislative experience when they arrived in the House and that another 29 percent had served only one previous term. Moreover, 159 members elected to the House in the period were students (law students, for instance) with little time for legislative work; of these, 108 had had no previous legislative experience.[41] With low pay and inadequate staffing, turnover is common; the result is that in the legislator-lobbyist relationship, it is the lobbyist, not the legislator, who is the experienced, skilled technician in lawmaking.

This generalization on the impact of legislative amateurism on lobbying deserves some qualification. In the Texas Senate, the rate of turnover has not been as high as in the House. Those senators with long tenure have been able to achieve considerable influence over the legislative process. Lobbyists recognize this and seek access to such senators. And in the House, the few members who remain to build tenure also figure prominently in the plans of lobbyists as important points of access. Such influential senators and representatives may be able to counter lobbyists' pressure—if, of course, they have not become spokesmen for vested interests long before.

Forty states make at least a token effort to regulate lobbying. Of these, 31 require the registration of legislative agents and their hired counsel, and 25 states require financial reports as well; nine states do nothing more than regulate improper lobbying activities. The general intent of state laws is to make the activities of lobbyists visible in the vain hope that public awareness will temper them. Texas also requires registration and financial reporting, but there, as in other states, the regulation is more symbolic than tangible. Ambiguities, contradictions, and a general lack of enforcement typify regulation everywhere. The result is that legal restraints offer little hindrance to interests using lobbying as a preferred technique.

---

[41]William E. Oden, "Tenure and Turnover in Recent Texas Legislatures," *Southwestern Social Science Quarterly,* 45 (March 1965), pp. 371-74; William E. Oden, "Some Characteristics of Recent Texas Legislators," *Rocky Mountain Social Science Journal,* IV (October, 1967), pp. 110-19.

## DEMAND POLITICS IN TEXAS

This description of how political demands are articulated and pressed by organized interests in Texas has probably raised more questions than it has provided answers to existing questions. We can say now, for example, that the basic pattern of demand politics in Texas is that of a loose alliance of dominant, established interests that exercise a veto over major changes threatening entrenched privileges. But we still have no accurate measure of the size of this establishment; nor are there any systematic case analyses of which interests exercise crucial influence in specific policy areas, let alone objective studies of any wider, more pervasive, political domination by the establishment.[42] Similarly, we know that there are large minorities in Texas consisting of the young, the impoverished, the blacks, and the Mexican-Americans, who scarcely have any voice at all in pressure politics. But, once more, we have no evidence of the potential for organization among these elements that would permit us to forecast the impact of their future entry into the politics of interest groups. Finally, we have described some of the ways in which established interests have been able to institutionalize privilege, participate actively in political campaigns, and lobby on their own behalf. However, while studies of the relations between organized interests and policy-makers yield clues about the possible effects of interest-group activity in various states, the absence of systematic inquiry into that facet of Texas politics denies us knowledge of how demands originating in the environment are successfully pressed in the Texas political system.

On the basis of the evidence that is available, we must hypothesize that demand politics in Texas is the politics of established interests. To the extent that this is so, it is merely additional evidence that the Texas political system is embedded in the type of traditionalistic-individualistic political culture described in Chapter 3. Several factors contribute to the influence that pressure groups have in Texas — the predominantly one-party system; the insulation of decision-makers from popular electoral control by detailed constitutional protections; the quality of amateurism in legislative politics; the protectionist (veto) strategy of dominant interests, silently supported by middle-class interests through the party, electoral, educational, and communications systems; and the widespread indifference to things political among the mass of lower middle-class and impoverished Texans.

Unlike the situation in many of the older, more stable, state polities of the eastern United States, organized interests in Texas did not have to fight public officials for recognition. Rather, the established Texas interests actually shared in the founding and development of the state's political

---

[42]See, however, Irving Owen Dawson, "The Texas State Teachers Association and the Amendment 4 Campaign," *Southwest Social Science Quarterly*, 41 (December 1961), 424-33.

system. Lobbyists and policy-makers "grew up" together, with economic development in the state preceding and guiding political development. It is not surprising, therefore, that established interests were able to shape political institutions to their own liking. Interests that missed out on that economic development missed out on political representation as well. They were excluded from the pressure system — the least studied and least understood of all the subsystems of Texas politics, yet the prime filter through which all demands to which policy-makers respond must pass.

# POLITICAL OUTPUTS: POLICY-MAKING PROCESSES IN TEXAS

*PART THREE*

# 5

# Organizing The Conversion Process

In Part One we observed that political systems, in order to persist, must respond to stresses from their environments. They do this through a variety of overlapping processes, and we listed three such processes that lend themselves to study in the examination of state political systems—the input process, in which supports and demands originate; the conversion process, whereby these supports and demands are translated into gains for some interests and burdens for others; and the output process, which allocates costs and benefits to various elements of society. In Part Two we discussed the sources of supports and demands in Texas politics. To round out our understanding of the Texas political system, we shall examine in this chapter the institutions within which policy conversion occurs, and, in the following chapter, the activities resulting in the allocations of costs and benefits to Texans.

## THE CONVERSION PROCESS IN TEXAS: STRUCTURE AND ROLES

In discussing the nature of the conversion process of a political system, Chapter 1 emphasized that there is rarely a strictly organized, carefully planned, sequence of events translating social demands directly into public policies. Instead, the phases of policy conversion overlap; the authority and responsibility for policy-making are fragmented and diffused among a proliferation of sometimes collaborating and sometimes competing offices, agencies, and groups. We can sort out four phases of the conversion process that usually take place—*initiation* of policy demands, *bargaining* between various interests to achieve passage or rejection of proposals, *enforcement* (application) of officially accepted policies, and *feedbacks* (reactions to policy outputs) into the political system.

These phases—initiation, bargaining, enforcement, and feedback—characterize the conversion process in Texas. Indeed, a cursory examination of the Constitution of 1876 suggests that its drafters envisaged a tidy institutional scheme dividing these phases among separate "departments" of state government. To the Governor, for example, went the responsibility for initiating policy proposals; the Constitution decreed that "he shall recommend to the Legislature such measures as he may deem expedient." To the department impressively designated "The Legislature of the State of Texas" went, appropriately enough, the "legislative power," which we take to mean the authority to debate, bargain over, modify, and pass bills. The "Executive Department," which we interpret as responsible for enforcing and applying policies, was to consist of "a Governor, who shall be the chief executive officer of the State; a Lieutenant Governor, Secretary of State, Comptroller of Public Accounts, Treasurer, Commissioner of the General Land Office and Attorney General." Finally, to the "Judicial Department" fell the task of hearing cases challenging or in violation of standing laws.

Thus, in neat, clear language, beyond (one would think) misinterpretation, the Constitution of 1876 assigned the *roles* of Texas public officials. It will be recalled from Chapter 1 that in any system (political or otherwise) a role is a segment of a person's total behavior appropriate to interacting with others in that system; thus, the Constitution simply decreed the "appropriate" behavior for officials—some were to exercise policy leadership, others were to play the role of legislator, others were to be administrators, and others to serve as adjudicators. "And," entoned the Constitution, "no person, or collection of persons, being of one of these departments shall exercise any power properly attached to either of the others, except in the instances herein expressly permitted."

But this simplest of all role allocations was never attained in practice. Instead, as in all operating political systems, roles were shaped by how each individual conceived he should behave in particular situations and by the ways others suggested he should behave. Hence, legislators, jealous of their prerogatives to debate, modify, and pass laws, added the initiation of proposals to their role-playing repertoire. Lesser executive officials elected independently of the Governor (such as the Lieutenant Governor or Attorney General) deemed themselves responsible not to the constitutionally designated "chief executive officer of the State" (the Governor), but to their separate constituencies. With aplomb, some successfully challenged the Governor for policy leadership (as did Lieutenant Governor Preston Smith, presiding officer of the Senate, in a feud with Governor John Connally in the 1960s that embittered senate-gubernatorial relations). And Governors, challenged by ambitious legislators and "insubordinate" executive subordinates, sought popular and partisan support, thus adding the roles of popular persuader and party leader to those of initiator and chief executive officer. Finally, to confuse the superficially tidy constitutional picture even more come the roles of persons not even mentioned in the Constitution of 1876, the lobbying spokesmen for established interests who initiate, bargain over, and reject any policy proposals.

Thus, we cannot rely upon simple constitutional designations of who the role participants are in the Texas conversion process, nor can we accept without question the formal description of the relations between those that are designated. Instead, we shall endeavor to specify the roles actually played, which intertwine the Governor, legislature, and other authorities in policy-making, Texas style.

## THE GUBERNATORIAL ROLE: INITIATOR OR STANDPATTER?

Thinking back over his tenure as Governor of Texas (1949-1957), Allan Shivers wrote, "The Governor of Texas is something of a paper tiger. The traditions and trappings of such a high office promise more real power for the Governor than has been provided under our still viable Constitution of 1876." He added, however, that "if an impression has been created that the Governor of Texas is without influence in the state government, it should be corrected at once."[1]

Contained in this statement, and in others like it made by several Texans, is the belief that the Governor of Texas possesses influence in the political system, yet not sufficient authority to control policy-making. This lack of authority gives some governors an excuse to accomplish very little during their incumbencies; they offer no legislative program, make no appeals, and serve only as prestigious heads of state. They play in short, the role of the standpatter. Others, however, take such authority as is available, combine it with personal and partisan popularity, and act as initiators— offering gubernatorial programs, building coalitions, and working on legislative strategies. In point of fact, any governor has sufficient constitutional authority to do more than stand pat, but he must have other sources of

---

[1]Allan Shivers, "The Governor's Office in Retrospect," in *Governing Texas: Documents and Readings,* eds. Fred Gantt, Jr., Irving Owen Dawson, and Luther G. Hagard, Jr. (New York: Thomas Y. Crowell Co., 1966), pp. 145, 147.

authority if he is truly to be an initiator in the conversion process. Let us examine these formal and informal influences on the gubernatorial role.

## THE EXECUTIVE AUTHORITY OF THE GOVERNOR

The formal powers of the Governor of Texas have not changed in their essentials since the adoption of the present Constitution.[2] Basically, they are derived from his tenure and his control over appointments to public office. As the chief elective executive official, the Governor of Texas serves a two-year term; there is no limitation to the number of terms to which he may be elected, yet a three-term maximum has become a tradition in the political culture. By the end of the 1960s, Texas was one of only 11 states in the United States utilizing a two-year rather than a four-year gubernatorial term. Although less restrictive in this regard than New Mexico or South Dakota (both restrict their Governors to two two-year terms), Texans were reluctant to permit four-year gubernatorial terms, with or without provision for reelection. In keeping with the traditionalistic-individualistic character of the political culture, Texans as recently as 1965 rejected a proposal for a four-year term at the polls.

A two-year term, despite possibilities of reelection, tends to work against executive control of the administrative bureaucracy. Persons appointed by the Governor, such as members of boards and commissions enjoying six-year terms, are likely to serve longer in office than he. In general, therefore, it is not unusual to find that those officials most loyal and sensitive to the Governor's wishes are those he appoints while those appointed by a predecessor are less likely to support his program.

Although the Governor has the authority to appoint persons to state boards and commissions, thus giving him some possibility of influencing their actions, this appointive power is shared with the Texas Senate. Appointments are made with the advice and consent of two-thirds of that body. In practice, the Governor obtains the approval of any senator from a potential appointee's home district; this is the custom of "senatorial courtesy." Should he fail to obtain that consent and press the appointment anyway, the senator who finds the appointee objectionable may request the entire Senate to reject the appointment. Any governor offering a program seriously at odds with senate interests, therefore, finds it difficult to obtain administrative subordinates sympathetic to his administration, even though he is the "chief executive."

---

[2]Fred Gantt, Jr., *The Chief Executive in Texas* (Austin: The University of Texas Press, 1964), pp. 36-39.

The Governor's influence over the executive establishment is further diminished by the fact that many executive officials are elected, not appointed. Thus, the Governor announces his programs independently of, and sometimes without reference to, the administrative officials who themselves seek elective office. It should also be noted that the Governor's appointive powers are shared with these elected administrative heads. Thus, administrators possess their own patronage, and their appointees are bound to them as well as to the Governor.[3] Such elected administrators have the opportunity to build up their own followings, serving several terms in office and watching many governors come and go. There is little compulsion for elected administrators to follow gubernatorial dictates or support gubernatorial initiative. Indeed, they may seek to exert their own initiative in the conversion process by articulating their own demands and goals, perhaps seeing themselves as eventual contenders for the gubernatorial role. The Attorney General, for instance, is especially likely to have public differences with the Governor, since, by tradition at least, his office is a major stepping-stone to the governorship.

There is relatively little that a governor can do to strengthen his hand against recalcitrant administrative subordinates, appointed or elected. As is the case with governors in most states, the Governor of Texas has virtually no authority to remove appointed officials other than members of his own staff or very minor officials.[4] With respect to elected administrators, there are rare occasions when a governor has appealed to voters to elect a candidate of his choice. But such appeals seldom convince voters. In 1938, for example, W. Lee O'Daniel, having won the gubernatorial nomination in the first party primary, asked voters to elect four candidates for other offices in the second primary who would support his program. Two of the four lost election, and it is questionable that O'Daniel's endorsement really contributed to the victories of the other two.[5]

Clearly, then, the executive authority of the "chief" executive is restricted in several ways—by limited tenure, nonexclusive appointive powers, virtually no power of removal, and the presence of rival elected executives. It should be stressed, however, that Texas is not alone in placing such restrictions on the executive authority of the Governor. A recent survey of state governors and their principal staff members reveals that there is widespread feeling in all state political systems that gubernatorial prerogatives should

---

[3]Alan J. Wyner, "Gubernatorial Relations with Legislators and Administrators," *State Government*, 31 (Summer 1968), 199-203.

[4]Byron R. Abernethy, *Some Persisting Questions Concerning the Constitutional State Executive* (Lawrence, Kansas: Governmental Research Center of the University of Kansas, 1960), pp. 50-58.

[5]Gantt, *The Chief Executive in Texas*, p. 113.

be strengthened. Two-thirds of the respondents, for example, mentioned the lack of sufficient appointive authority as a major weakness in the gubernatorial office; more than one-fourth worried about the shortness of gubernatorial terms; and, almost one-half felt Governors should have greater authority to reorganize their executive establishments.[6]

But to say that Texas is like other states in its restrictions upon gubernatorial executive authority is to gloss over the relative severity of Texas restrictions. When the appointive powers, tenure potential, budget powers, and veto powers of governorships in the United States in the 1960s are compared, Texas ranks with Mississippi, South Carolina, and North Dakota as being the most restrictive of all states in hamstringing the executive (and legislative) authorities of the Governor. Very much in keeping with the traditionalistic and individualistic elements of their political culture discussed in Chapter 2, Texans today maintain a nineteenth century attitude toward the governorship. In 1876, fearing that gubernatorial discretion would lead to repression—as it had during the Reconstruction Era—Texans fixed strict constitutional limits on the Governor's authority. Given such limitations, it is not too surprising that the average Texas Governor today finds it easier to play the role of standpatter than initiator in the conversion process.[7]

## THE LEGISLATIVE AUTHORITY OF THE GOVERNOR

If a Governor is to take the initiative in converting social demands into policy outputs, he must be active in the legislative arena as well as the executive. The Governor of Texas attempts to exert legislative influence through his official messages, budgetary authority, calling of special sessions, veto power, and selective strategy.

To the extent that a Governor wishes to obtain statewide publicity for his program, the Constitution provides him with a vehicle by requiring him to give the Texas legislature information about the condition of the state.

---

[6]Thad L. Beyle, "The Governor's Formal Powers: A View from the Governor's Chair," *Public Administration Review*, 28 (November-December 1968), 543. On the general tendency to restrict governors, see H. Alton Burdine, "Trends in Public Administration in the South," *Journal of Politics*, 10 (August 1948), 419-40; Cortez A. M. Ewing, "Southern Governors," *Journal of Politics*, 10 (May 1948), 384; Robert B. Highsaw, "The Southern Governor—Challenge to the Strong Executive Theme," *Public Administration Review*, 19 (1959); J. Alton Burdine, "Toward a More Effective Administration," *Texas Law Review*, 35 (October 1957), 939.

[7]Joseph A. Schlesinger, "The Politics of the Executive," in *Politics in the American States*, eds. Herbert Jacobs and Kenneth Vines (Boston: Little, Brown and Company, 1965), pp. 223-29.

He must do so, by message, at the opening of each legislative session and at the close of his term in office. Moreover, he must present his plans for the state budget within five days of the opening of the regular legislative session. As a result, it is customary for the Governor to prepare and deliver, with full coverage by the mass media, an address in which he transmits what he considers to be the most pressing social demands—those demands most in keeping with his program and his concept of desirable public policy. Subsequently, if he wishes to retain the initiative, he submits to the legislature written messages on major demands—pollution control, education, taxation, etc.—and specific legislative proposals for each. In effect, the message power is the power of publicity, a method for calling attention to major issues and for communicating gubernatorial desires to the legislature. However, there is no assurance that what the Governor proposes, the legislature will dispose.

As noted above, one of the Governor's messages concerns the budget. The most crucial period for any executive, public or private, is when he submits a budget for the operation of the organization for which he is responsible. Here his competence as a politician and administrator is tested. Here programs are first put into operation. Here are announced the priorities of the executive. And here, finally, the seeds are sown for the next campaign.

In Texas, the budgetary function is shared by many agencies and the Governor has only limited fiscal and budgetary control. Not only does the Legislative Budget Board submit a competing budget for all agencies of the state, but agencies themselves challenge the Governor's budget also with budgets of their own, some of which are only partial budgets and accounts for fiscal and tax administration handed down by the Treasurer, the Comptroller of Public Accounts, the State Board of Controls, and the State Auditor. Budgetary control is further diminished by constitutional stipulations earmarking taxes and the manner in which money can be spent. The Constitution contains specific stipulations establishing what may be taxed (products, articles, etc.) and limiting the purposes and rates of state appropriations. Hence, both the Governor and the legislature are constitutionally restricted in their taxing and spending authority. (We shall examine the function of the budgetary process in allocating costs and benefits among Texans in greater detail in Chapter 6.)

Regular sessions of the Texas legislature are held every two years, on the odd-numbered year, for a maximum of 140 days. Special sessions, however, may be called by the Governor; each such session may last for no longer than thirty days. Not only may the Governor call special sessions, but he may also specify topics to be considered. In the less than a century since the adoption of the 1876 Constitution, 21 of the 25 Governors have called a combined total of 72 special sessions. While some Governors have called the sessions to obtain desired legislation, others have simply threatened sessions in hopes of obtaining action on proposals during the regular session from legislators not desirous of making another trip to Austin. In recent years, the calling of a special session has been urged upon Governors by some state leaders as a method of dealing more effectively with budgetary problems. It is now impossible, so goes the argument, for a legislature meeting once every two years to raise and appropriate money for state government to operate on for two years; combining the biennial regular session with a special budget session in the off year would permit annual budgetary action. Governor John Connally employed the special session for such a purpose in 1968. Governor Preston Smith, however, refused to live by such an arrangement in his administration and recalled legislators following their regular session in 1969, demanding that they complete a two-year, not a one-year, budget, in contradiction to the proposal of the presiding officer of the Senate, Lieutenant Governor Ben Barnes.

Combined with careful timing of sessions, selection of agenda topics, and negotiations with legislative leaders, the power to call special sessions would seem to give the Governor a significant role in the legislative aspect of policy conversion. His influence, however, is not as great as might first appear. For one thing, there is no assurance that the legislature will act at all on the topics for which the session was called; thus, the Governor must either forget his program or call yet another session. In addition, Governors themselves realize that taxpayers may not be eager to pay the costs of innumerable special sessions (legislators collect $30 a day for each of the 30 days). Finally, a legislature in session can be a source of opposition and dissent as well as one of support; some Governors therefore prefer to let sleeping dogs lie.

The Governor of Texas, like other Governors, has the authority to veto legislation. Acts passed by the Texas legislature must be sent to the Governor for approval; should he not approve an act or acts, he must announce his veto within 10 days of their presentation to him (or within 20 days of legislative adjournment, if the session has ended). Moreover, as in 41 other states, the Governor may veto individual items in appropriation bills while approving the remaining sections (the "item veto"). He may not, however, reduce finances for certain items in the appropriations bill or delete instructions for expenditures.

The veto authority is one of the Governor's most significant controls over prospective legislation, for there is a hesitancy to pass legislation which the Governor will clearly find objectionable. To override the gubernatorial veto, two-thirds of the members present in each legislative house must vote to do so. Such cases are rare; indeed, fewer than one in ten gubernatorial vetoes have been overridden since 1876, and none in the last three decades.

While the veto is a potent tool, however, it must be recognized that it is one by which a Governor is more likely to preserve the status quo than seek initiative for change. Through the veto he can prevent what he does not like, but cannot recommend or propose the legislation he prefers. The veto does, of course, permit the Governor to bargain with legislative interests by promising legislators not to veto their pet projects if they will support his program. But—as in the case of his message powers, budget authority, and prerogatives to call special sessions—the veto power cannot be used indiscriminately. A Governor who wishes to retain the initiative in the conversion process must, because of his limited constitutional options, practice a selective strategy. Proper timing, adroit bargaining, careful filtering of demands, and personal influence must be substituted for executive and legislative authority. He must, in short, cultivate extralegal support if he is to process demands effectively in the role of initiator rather than standpatter.

## THE PERSONAL STYLE OF THE GOVERNOR

Each Governor adds his personal style to the powers he derives from the Constitution, and each style tends to be unique. Thus, one Governor may be weak, another a "do-nothing clerk," and another an active, aggressive reformer. His style of playing the gubernatorial role is determined by several factors—his social characteristics, the degree of partisan control during his incumbency, his powers of persuasion, his personality and popularity, and his orientation to the demands made upon him.

The evidence indicates that from the standpoint of social characteristics the typical man elected Governor of Texas is reasonably young (around 47 years of age), has attended college, probably is a lawyer, has been in public life for several years (generally with experience in state, rather than federal or local government), comes from a relatively small city, is a native-born Texan, and is intent on serving two terms. He is likely to be (in recent years) a member of a veterans' organization, married, and a Protestant.[8] He may have future political ambitions, but so prestigious is the office that he is probably capping his career by gubernatorial service. Indeed, in recent years a United States senator (Price Daniel), an ambassador (Ed Clark), a secretary of the Navy (John Connally), and other ranking officials have returned to Texas just to have the opportunity to run for, and hopefully play, the gubernatorial role.

Of course, the Governor of Texas is the nominal, and sometimes the effective, leader of his political party. To the extent that the party is a viable, highly disciplined institution, the Governor has the opportunity to achieve legislative unity behind his program by exerting his partisan leadership. But

---

[8]Gantt, *The Chief Executive in Texas*, pp. 36-39.

there are two difficulties here. As noted in Chapter 3, the dominant Democratic party is faction-ridden, relatively poorly disciplined, and not an effective instrument for influencing policy-making. And as far as the Republicans are concerned, should their candidate win the governorship, he would find few loyal partisans in the largely Democratic legislature on whom to call for program support. Like his Democratic opponent, he would need to forge a coalition of established interests that would restrain any impulse he might have to work major policy changes in the faction-ridden traditionalistic political system.

The capacity to persuade is a major asset to any Governor seeking the policy-making initiative. In part, the office itself provides the occupant with certain resources for persuasion. A request for action from the Governor of Texas carries with it a mystique and symbolism not matched by the demand of a private citizen. By virtue of his office, the Governor speaks for TEXAS, or at least there is that assumption when he makes an appeal by message, public appearance, or televised address. By appealing to the constituents of a member of the legislature, he may bring pressure to bear for a much-needed vote. One of the first Governors to make such public appeals through the mass media was W. Lee O'Daniel. Once master of ceremonies for a singing group called the Light Crust Doughboys, O'Daniel founded a flour company, Hillbilly Flour, and used its band (the Hillbilly Band) for broad campaign appeals.

The personality of the Governor also contributes to his powers of persuasion. To the extent that he was able to influence the conversion process in the 1960s, for example, Governor John Connally owed much to his remarkable popularity among Texans. Four months after his inauguration in 1963, Connally received the approval of 54 percent of the Texans surveyed on his conduct as Governor; seven months later the figure had risen to 79 percent. Similarly, Govenor Allen Shivers, after eight months in office in 1950, received the approval of 76 percent of the Texans surveyed. In contrast, the percentage of Texans favoring Governor Preston Smith's performance fell from 54 percent in March 1969 two months after taking office to 48 percent three months later.[9] It is unknown whether Governor Smith sought to seize the initiative for policy changes in those months, but to the extent that he might have it would have been difficult to achieve in the face of his declining popularity.

The stance a Governor takes toward the social demands fed into the political system is determined in part by his social background, persuasiveness, and popularity. It begins to emerge when he becomes a candidate for office, becomes clarified in the course of the campaign, and sharpens once his

---

[9]Joe Belden, "The Texas Poll," *The Dallas Morning News*, June 22, 1969.

incumbency begins. It includes the places he looks for issues, the direction in which he formulates his goals, the sources he uses for information, and the people he trusts.

Among the principal demands made on the most Texas Governors are those emanating from the economic system. The oil industry, for example, has always sought to avoid tax burdens on grounds that the state must enable it to compete with out-of-state oil interests and on the world market. But there have been demands on Governors from the broader social system as well—equal rights for women, relaxed divorce laws, less restrictive abortion statutes, social welfare legislation, etc.

Thus, it is from varied sources that a gubernatorial candidate chooses issues and formulates policies which he hopes will win votes in party primaries and the general election. By selecting and articulating issues and proposing their solutions, the candidate structures the demands to be placed before officials. John Connally, for example, formulated a program to expand higher education; once he was elected, his program became part of the demands he placed before the legislature. He related this program to the economic system by contending that more industry would locate in Texas as the quality of higher education improved. Other Governors have tried to create demands favorable to business: Allan Shivers in the 1950s stressed the cost of a labor strike upon businesses in Port Arthur by circulating the *Port Arthur Story*, an anti-labor brochure. Wilbur Lee O'Daniel's campaign platform was to get "politics out of government and put business in." In such cases the candidate articulates some of the needs, desires, or fears of selected interests and offers them as a meaningful set of demands.

Where the candidate gets his information contributes much to his selection of demands. That a candidate might turn to personal friends is not unexpected. That he might also turn to a group of previous winners, or to those who have controlled political decisions, is understandable. In fact, these seem to be common sources of information everywhere, particularly in countries with traditional political cultures. There the modern political party with mass support has not supplanted the coterie of friends, but has combined with it.[10] The exact mixture of reliance in Texas upon the mass party is not known, but winning candidates have probably relied more upon the coterie.

For an incumbent, the gubernatorial staff is a principal source of information. It channels demands, writes legislative proposals, pours forth press releases, and projects the image of an effective leader. Compared to gubernatorial staffs of the nineteenth century, those of recent years have

---

[10] Gabriel A. Almond and James S. Coleman, *The Politics of Developing Areas* (Princeton University Press, 1960), p. 21.

been sizable. Governor James Hogg's staff in 1890 consisted of a "private secretary, a stenographic clerk, and a porter." Compare this with the 80-person staff of Governor John Connally in the 1960s.[11]

We can summarize this discussion of the gubernatorial role in the conversion process by emphasizing that it is severely curtailed by the Constitution. The Governor's authority over executive establishment is anemic, and his influence with the legislature is dependent primarily upon good public relations, partisan harmony, and the threat of the veto. If he is to have the initiative, he must work in consort with the principal established interests currently represented through the demand process. He does this chiefly through the party system and by working with legislative leaders. If, however, he envisions himself as a champion of hitherto unrepresented interests —black or white, old or young, affluent or impoverished, rural or urban—he will have a hard time formulating a program, obtaining the support of his administrative subordinates (appointed or elective), and winning the approval of legislative interests. As structured by the Constitution of 1876, the governorship is less likely to be a center for stimulating change in the Texas political system than a prestigious preserver of the status quo.

# THE LEGISLATIVE ROLE: POLICY DELIBERATION IN TEXAS POLITICS

If there is a point in the conversion process in Texas where influence generally rests, that point is probably the Texas legislature. Through relations with lobbying interests, through its leadership structure, and through its committee process, the Texas legislature plays many roles in policy conversion—initiation, bargaining, application, and feedback. To obtain an idea of the nature of legislative politics in Texas, we must look at the legislative subsystem and its authority.

### THE LEGISLATIVE SYSTEM IN TEXAS

Legislatures, as we noted in Chapter 1, are miniature systems in their own right which act as subsystems within more overarching political systems. As institutions whose members are the directly elected representatives of the state's citizens, legislatures ideally serve as microcosms of the population and act on behalf of all citizens in the conversion process. Legis-

---

[11]Gantt, *The Chief Executive in Texas,* pp. 96-104; Coleman Ransone, *The Office of Governor in the United States* (University, Alabama: University of Alabama Press, 1956), pp. 302-62.

latures formulate policies by initiating proposals, debating them, modifying them through bargaining and compromise, and accepting or rejecting them through final vote. In order that state legislative bodies can perform these functions, constitutions traditionally designate to them certain formal powers—to legislate in defined social areas, to carry on investigations, to organize their own affairs, to carry out specified judicial and impeachment proceedings with regard to their own members and other state officials, and to propose constitutional amendments. By converting, reducing, and integrating demands and building support for its policy outputs, a legislature serves as a major link between the political system and its diverse environments. The extent to which a legislature lives up to this idealized role, and thus truly reflects the diverse interests of all the state's citizenry, depends upon many factors, including the legislature's structure and rules, its internal organization and leadership, and its composition.

## The Structure and Rules of the Texas Legislative Subsystem

Like all states except Nebraska, Texas has two houses in its legislature. The lower house, the House of Representatives, consists of 150 members elected for a term of two years. The upper house, the Senate, consists of 31 members who serve four-year staggered terms. A five-year residence in the state is required of senators, and a two-year residence of representatives. A senator must be at least 26 years of age, and a representative at least 21; each must be a citizen of the United States and a qualified voter.

Although all 31 senators in Texas are elected from single-member districts, 88 of the members of the lower house are elected from 18 multi-member districts (that is, constituencies having more than one representative). By legal requirement, any single senator must represent approximately the same number of constituents as any other (the "one man, one vote" principle); the same holds true for house members. However, it was not until the late 1960s that legislative districts were apportioned so as to provide for equal populations within each. In contemporary Texas, as in other states, the effect of such reapportionment has been to increase the formal representation of urban and suburban interests. It remains to be seen, however, what impact equal districting will have on the conversion process in the 1970s.

By and large, the same rules and privileges exist for members of both legislative houses. Each house sits in judgment on the qualifications of its own members and adopts its own rules. In each house, members are free from arrest during a legislative session except in cases of treason, felony, or breach of peace; immunity from prosecution is constitutionally granted for what is said in debate. The Texas Constitution has a conflict-of-interest clause which stipulates that "a member who has a personal or private interest in any measure or bill, proposed or pending before the Legislature, shall declare the fact to the house of which he is a member, and shall not vote therein." The effectiveness of this provision depends either upon open declaration by the member involved or upon another member indicating that member's involvement, thereby forcing his declaration and compelling him to withdraw from participating in the legislative decision. Traditionally, the provision is enforced through open declaration, in a reliance on good faith and mutual trust.

There are a series of constitutional constraints upon legislative operations: a bill must have readings on three separate days, except in cases of imperative public necessity; revenue bills must originate in the House of Representatives; no bill may contain more than one subject; no bill may be considered unless it has been referred to a committee and reported on at least three days before adjournment.

The Constitution further requires that there be a "split session," which allocates certain legislative business to certain time periods. The first 30 days are devoted to the introduction of bills, emergency appropriations, and other special business; the next 30 days are devoted to committee hearings; and the last 60 days are devoted to consideration and debate on legislative measures. In 1876 these requirements were intended to protect Texans against capricious and arbitrary legislative action. The citizen was to follow proceedings and know that if a bill was not introduced during the first period it would not come before the legislature. These restrictions can be avoided, however, because Article III, Section 5 of the Constitution provides that "either house may otherwise determine its order of business by an affirmative vote of four-fifths of its membership." Both houses have indeed "otherwise determined" in their respective rules.

## Internal Organization and Legislative Leadership

With a few exceptions, the two houses of the Texas Legislature are empowered by the Constitution to determine their own organization and leadership. These exceptions include the designation of the Lieutenant Governor as the presiding officer of the Senate (allowed to cast a vote to break ties) and the definition of a quorum as two-thirds of each house's members. The Constitution permits each house to compel attendance of members, to punish them for rule violations, and to expel members by consent of two-thirds of the house's membership. Each body is required to keep a journal recording its proceedings.

The principal organizational device for legislative affairs is the committee structure. Committees act as mechanisms for transferring the arena of battle from the whole body to a smaller group. There the merits are argued and the general fate of a measure is determined. Since by constitutional stipulation all bills must be referred to a committee, the committees are a very important part of the legislative process.

There are three types of committee: standing, select, and conference. Each house has 24 standing (permanent) committees and the right to create an indefinite number of select (temporary) committees. Conference committees are appointed to deliberate and resolve differences between the houses on particular legislation. In each instance, committee members are appointed by the presiding officer of the respective legislative body, the Speaker in the case of the House of Representatives and the Lieutenant Governor in the case of the Senate. The fact that the Lieutenant Governor, a separately elected executive official, has appointive power in the Senate gives him considerable leverage in the conversion process, within both the legislative and executive establishments.

The Speaker of the House is elected by house members for a two-year term. The position is the focal point of leadership in the House. Not only does the Speaker exercise the power of appointing committee members, but he also recognizes legislators in floor debate, interprets rules, refers bills to committees, guides legislation through the House, and works closely with all house officers. These powers, plus the prestige of the office, make the election of the Speaker a contest of more than passing concern not only to house members but to lobbyists, the Governor, and all state officials. Speakers in recent years have used their position as a stepping-stone to more notable achievements: Waggoner Carr moved from the speakership to election as Attorney General in 1962; Byron Tunnell was appointed to the Railroad Commission after his speakership in 1963; Ben Barnes was elected Lieutenant Governor after his service as speaker in 1968; and Gus Mutscher made the most publicized conquest of all, marrying a former Miss America after being elected speaker!

Since the Lieutenant Governor is also the presiding officer of the Senate, the general election determines who is to preside over that body. The powers of the Lieutenant Governor are the same as those of the speaker. He staffs the senate committees, for instance, thereby having a strong influence on the type of legislation adopted by the Senate. However, the Lieutenant Governor has powers which the speaker does not have.[12] He is, for example, chairman of the powerful Legislative Budget Board, which consists of the Speaker of the House of Representatives, four house appointees (including

---

[12] J. William Davis, *There Shall Also Be A Lieutenant Governor* (Austin: Institute of Public Affairs of the University of Texas, 1967).

the chairmen of the Revenue and Taxation Committee and the Appropriation Committee), and four senators appointed by the Lieutenant Governor (including the chairmen of the Finance Committee and the Senate Affairs Committee). The existence of the Legislative Budget Board testifies to the built-in conflict between the legislative and executive branches and to the belief that budgeting is a legislative prerogative and function and not an executive one. Since the leader and powerful committee chairmen of both houses are on the board, the two bodies are more prone to support the board than to go with the Governor's recommendation on the budget. Thus, the Governor's role in the conversion process is diminished all the more.

## Legislative Role-Players

In recent years political scientists have displayed considerable curiosity about the persons who campaign for and are elected to legislative seats in state political systems.[13] As a result, there are studies of the legislative role-players of at least one-fourth of the states. These studies cover such items as the social background of the legislator, his views on his position, and his aspirations. When we compare what we know of Texas legislators with such studies, we find that the typical Texas lawmaker does not differ a great deal from his counterpart in other states. For instance, investigations indicate that most state legislators, whatever state they are from, have more years of formal education than the general population (over 50 percent of legislators are college graduates), that most are in professional or managerial occupations (lawyers dominate), and that they reflect the proportion of the various religious denominations of their states. Much the same holds for Texas: about two-thirds of recent Texas legislators have been college graduates; 40 percent of the house members and 69 percent of the senators have been lawyers (25 percent of the house members have been businessmen, compared to only 12 percent of the senators); and more than two-thirds of the house and senate members come from Protestant backgrounds.[14]

State legislators define their roles in various ways. Some are ritualists, concerned with making laws by mastering technical rules, legislative routine, and parliamentary practices. Others are tribunes, perceiving their basic function as the direct representation of their constituents' interests.

---

[13]See John C. Wahlke, Heinz Eulau, William Buchanan, and LeRoy C. Ferguson, *The Legislative System* (New York: John Wiley and Sons, Inc., 1962); James David Barber, *The Lawmakers* (New Haven: Yale University Press, 1965); Harmon Zeigler and Michael Baer, *Lobbying: Interaction and Influence in American State Legislatures* (Belmont, Cal.: Wadsworth Publishing Co., 1969); and Frank J. Sorauf, *Party and Representation* (New York: Atherton Press, 1962).

[14]William E. Oden, "Some Characteristics of Recent Texas Legislators," *The Rocky Mountain Social Science Journal*, 4 (October 1967), 110-19.

Still others are inventors, exploring new solutions to old problems of taxation, welfare, pollution, etc. And finally there are the brokers, who see their job as resolving conflict between diverse interests having legislative access.[15] We can speculate that Texas has a large share of brokers (working closely with lobbying interests), several ritualists among its committee chairmen, fewer tribunes, and not many inventors.

With regard to legislators' career aspirations, we might again speak of four types: lawmakers, who are very active in the work of the legislature and desire to return for several terms; spectators, who wish to serve for several legislative terms but take relatively little part in legislative business; advertisers, who serve actively for but one or two legislative terms in order to build a reputation and thus gain higher office; and reluctants, who care little about legislative work and wish to leave the legislature as soon as their term ends. The likelihood seems to be that in Texas we will find more lawmakers in the Senate than in the House (on the average, 47 percent of the senators, but only 11 percent of the representatives, have had four or more years of legislative experience) and both more reluctants and more advertisers in the House (nearly 40 percent of the representatives are freshman legislators, indicating a relatively high average turnover).[16]

### PROCESSES OF LEGISLATIVE CONVERSION

In Texas the legislature organizes itself to maintain the initiative in the consideration of demands, bargains with lobbyists (recall Chapter 4) and within committees to achieve workable compromises, and attempts to exert some control over enforcement in the conversion process.

## Legislative Initiative: Estimating Committee Action

For a person to run for the legislature he must file as a candidate by February 2 of the election year. The first primary is held on the first Saturday in May, and if no majority is won the second on the first Saturday in June. The general election takes place on the first Tuesday after the first Monday in November. The legislator takes office in January, almost a full year after he has filed. He has campaigned on his own, securing such funds

---

[15]Wahlke et al., *The Legislative System*, pp. 245-60.
[16]Barber, *The Lawmakers*, p. 20; William E. Oden, "Tenure and Turnover in Recent Texas Legislatures," *Southwestern Social Science Quarterly*, 45 (March 1965), 371.

and endorsements as he can and making commitments as necessary or expedient. He has been busy structuring demands and supports for his causes and programs, and he has done this independently of the candidates for the governorship and other offices. If this is his first term in the lower house, he may arrive too late to be in on the decisions that matter about the election of the Speaker (since the winning candidate received a large portion of his promised votes as the last session ended). He has thus lost any bargaining leverage for choice committee appointments, and about the best he can hope for is to find a backer from among incumbent legislators to champion his cause. There are rare instances, however, when a freshman legislator may have a voice in the struggle over control of legislative conversions, and some battles are decided by the votes of the freshmen members (as, for instance, in the Carr-Burkett fight in 1959 and the Turman-Spilman contest in 1961).

Since the Speaker of the House appoints all members of house commitees, his campaign and election shape who will be on the committees and, hence, to a large degree what will come out of the committees. If a representative helped manage the Speaker's campaign or helped garner support for him, he may be able to count on a more important committee assignment (there is no rule of seniority in Texas, despite attempts to establish one). However, since the Speaker in seeking election has bargained with and made commitments to other legislators as well, the representative's assignment is problematic.

The method of appointing members to committees sacrifices one of the advantages of the committee. Turnover is so high that one-half of the chairmen of some of the more important committees are new members of the committee with no previous experience on that committee. Thus, the expertise and control over policy-making which veteran legislators are able to build up under the rule of seniority elsewhere is not always present in Texas. The method of appointment means also that house committees usually reflect the interests of the Speaker and senate committees the interests of the Lieutenant Governor. These two officers make all committee appointments, thus using their power to structure policy.

It would be hard to argue that a high degree of turnover in committee membership means a lack of leadership among legislators, since, almost by definition, those who are appointed are credited with leadership. However, it can be argued with a great deal of validity that the frequent changes in committee membership create a certain instability (which, for one thing, makes it extremely difficult for a neophyte to anticipate what a committee might do). This instability insures log-rolling (vote-trading), buttonholing, and brokerage. Thus, when a distinguished member is giving an impassioned speech on the chamber floor, an observer can witness other legislators roaming over the floor, forming small groups, exchanging information, and dissolving only to coalesce again with a new and different composition. This activity is referred to as "running traps" or "running my line." It becomes more feverish as the session nears its end. It is an attempt to touch base, to put in a last word, and to size up the situation in a disordered universe of unstable committees and coalitions.

The courses of action open to a legislative committee in Texas are approximately the same as those in the United States Congress. The committee can kill a bill, amend it, or even recommend that a substitute bill be accepted instead. The last alternative is possible even though the Constitution states that all bills must be referred to a committee. In this case a ruse is used in which the substitute bill is stapled to the original bill, thus keeping the original bill number and thereby allowing the legislature to consider the committee's recommendation. If a representative wants to get his bill passed, it is important that he get the bill referred to a favorable subcommittee and hold public hearings if necessary.

Committee deliberation does act as a filtering device. It reduces the number of bills to be heard. The number of bills introduced has increased steadily, and committees now have more work to do than they had ten years ago. Table 5-1 lists the number of bills introduced and bills passed for both houses during the sessions from 1961 to 1969.

Legislative committees are able to play a dominant role in Texas because they are the most cohesive units acting in the legislative process. There are no party caucuses or party whips to enforce party loyalties or maintain party discipline among legislators. About the only cohesion shown outside the committee system is generated in the race for the speakership, which usually boils down to a one-man race, and sometimes this cohesion carries on through the session. Reporters traditionally coin names for the cohesive group such as "Turmocrats" (those who voted for and with Speaker James Turman) and "Ben's Boys" (the supporters of Speaker Ben Barnes). There is little empirical study of legislative roll-call votes in Texas to indicate whether even this cohesion actually exists. However, former representative H. Dicken Cherry of Waco reports that the cohesion generated by the race for the speaker in 1961 appeared on twelve important pieces of legislation, where 70 percent of those who supported Turman for speaker voted together. Cherry also feels that the cohesion generated by the speaker's race was more important than the cohesion arising from a rural-urban split in the same legislative session.[17]

---

[17]H. Dicken Cherry, "Texas: Factions in a One-Party Setting," in *The Politics of Reapportionment*, ed. Malcolm E. Jewell (New York: Atherton Press, 1962), p. 123.

TABLE 5-1  Introduction and Passage of Legislation in Texas, 1961-1969

| Regular Session | House Bills | House Resolutions | Senate Bills | Senate Resolutions |
|---|---|---|---|---|
| 57th Legislature (1961) | | | | |
| Introduced | 1136 | 83 | 480 | 25 |
| Passed | 316 | 6 | 235 | 8 |
| 58th Legislature (1963) | | | | |
| Introduced | 1088 | 80 | 525 | 30 |
| Passed | 332 | 1 | 204 | 6 |
| 59th Legislature (1965) | | | | |
| Introduced | 1187 | 84 | 587 | 48 |
| Passed | 491 | 15 | 271 | 12 |
| 60th Legislature (1967) | | | | |
| Introduced | 1363 | 64 | 628 | 41 |
| Passed | 571 | 12 | 254 | 8 |
| 61st Legislature (1969) | | | | |
| Introduced | 1485 | 66 | 856 | 34 |
| Passed | 586 | 10 | 358 | 6 |

Source: Charles A. Schnabel, Secretary of the Texas Senate, personal communication, June 20, 1969.

## Legislative Bargaining: The Conference Committee

In legislative bargaining, the conference committee is extremely influential. When the two houses have passed different versions of the same bill, a conference committee is appointed to work out the differences. Historically, the sessions of the conference committee have been secret but they ceased to be in 1967 with the passage of the "Open Meeting Bill."

The membership of the conference committee is determined by the presiding officer in each house, who appoints five members from that body. These ten men write the final version of the bill. Actually, the committee consists of two committees acting in concert, since each group of five votes independently and then reports back to its own chamber.

The conference committee is free to act beyond the mere adjustment of differences, for it may consider matters that were not handled by either house during the session. Its recommendations cannot be amended; they must be accepted or rejected. If the conference committee is operating near the end of the session, it has an excellent chance for getting everything it wants regardless of the compromises and positions taken earlier by either house. Many legislators, confronted with a large document on a take it or leave it basis, simply put their faith in their colleagues and vote approval. On appropriation bills, riders may be attached, with no parliamentary method available for raising the question of relevance. To a large degree, those who control the conference committee control legislation; it is in the conference committee where the demands which have been put into the political system may be altered or stopped completely. As a former Texas legislator has written, the Texas legislature "doesn't legislate"; that is, the conference committee, not the houses representing citizens of Texas, controls policy conversion processes.[18]

It is obvious, then, that the legislators to influence are those who control the conference committee. These tend to be the senators, who by their greater artfulness and expertise generally overshadow the more inexperienced members from the House. Until the presiding officers no longer appoint chairmen and committee members, until the conference committees are restricted in their alternatives, until some seniority rules are adopted, and until the conference committee reports are made in sufficient time for consideration, or the 120-140 day limit to the session is removed, the process of legislative policy-making will be controlled largely by the dominant members of the conference committee and the presiding officers.

## Legislative Oversight: An Abortive Effort at Enforcement

In exercising legislative oversight, the legislative body scrutinizes the administrative branch and, through its power to investigate, confirm appointments, and control the purse strings, makes the executive render an accounting for its exercise of power. Certain practices and policies may be imposed upon the administration. Legislators may seek to compel administrators to adhere more closely to the law as the lawmakers see it, or they may ask that a given administrative rule or practice be changed. Oversight so practiced helps the legislator to engineer support for the political system by making it more accountable and more responsive to public demands. How effective is the legislature in performing this function in Texas?

In Texas, legislative oversight is barely rendered. One might say that it is honored less in the practice than the breach. Indeed, since the legislature meets for only 120 to 140 days, there probably can be little effective legislative inquiry into the conduct of the administration. Moreover, with tenure so low and turnover so high, and with such low salaries ($4800 per

---

[18]Cherry, "Texas: Factions in a One-Party Setting."

year plus $12 per diem for 120 days of the regular 140-day session), legislators are little inclined to make such inquiry. Finally, Texas legislators are not particularly well equipped to engage in overseeing a complex administrative establishment. Their clerical help is limited (four full-time secretaries for a senator, one full-time secretary for a representative); no full-time professional or administrative staff serves legislative leaders; and staff recruitment and training are particularly difficult because of low pay, the guarantee of employment for only a few months each biennium, and long hours of work when in session.

It might be argued that since administrative heads are elected, there is less need for legislative inquiry, as contenders for administrative posts themselves challenge each other to an accounting. But regular elections with short terms of office do not reduce the legislature's responsibility to publicize the crucial yet oft-ignored activities of the faceless role players in the conversion process.

## THE FACELESS ROLES: POLICY APPLICATION AND FEEDBACK

A Governor occupies a highly publicized, highly visible, and prestigious position in a state political system and, as we have noted, the Governor of Texas is no exception. Legislators, although not as visible as a Governor, are still thought of by citizens as officials of significance in policy-making. But there are two sets of role-players in state politics—administrators and judicial officers—who probably have more direct, day-to-day, impact upon the lives of citizens than either Governors or legislators. Their roles are seldom appreciated by the general public; indeed, few citizens pay much attention to either the administrator or judge until confronted with an onerous burden, such as paying a license fee or answering for some violation of the law, as when caught for speeding. Faceless as they may be as far as the citizenry is concerned, however, these role-players nonetheless warrant at least momentary consideration in our discussion of policy conversions in Texas.

### ADMINISTRATIVE AUTHORITY IN TEXAS

Like all states, Texas relies upon boards and commissions to carry out the day-by-day process of governing limited areas or functions. In most cases these boards are of three types: first, there are boards made up of elected authorities who, by virtue of office, are called upon to perform some collective governmental act; second, there are boards which carry out governmental functions and activities of a generic or broad type; and third, there are boards or commissions which reflect private interests and regulate a very small or narrow activity. An example of the first category is the State Tax Board, which is composed of the Comptroller, the Secretary of State, and the Attorney General. Examples of the second are the University of Texas Board of Regents and the Liquor Control Board. The last category, which includes by far the most agencies, is made up of private interests whose demands upon the system have been so successful that they have been awarded economic protection. (Both the demands and the awards are made, of course, in the name of the public welfare.) Examples, to name just a few, are the State Board of Barber Examiners, the State Board of Dental Examiners, the State Board of Hairdressers and Cosmetologists, and the Texas State Board of Medical Examiners—all economic interests which determine professional requirements. By limiting the number of people allowed to enter the profession, such agencies help establish the price the profession receives for its services.

There are more than 150 of these agencies, boards, or commissions operating in Texas. They are created by legislative statute, and their members are appointed by the Governor with the consent of the Senate. Thus, with membership on these boards averaging six or seven, the Governor appoints nearly 1000 people to help run the state. The terms of service are generally staggered, so that only one-third will be appointed in any given two-year period.

The significant aspect of the administrative establishment in Texas, however, is not that there are numerous units performing varied functions. Rather, there are two more noteworthy points. First, the very fact that Texas employs boards and commissions, rather than hierarachically structured agencies with a single official responsible for operations, is instructive. The diffusion of responsibility for board policies among a number of individuals provides multiple points of access for interests concerned with establishing privilege, securing it, and expanding it in the future. This permits special interests to play a major role in the enforcement and application of policies and, in effect, to make direct demands not only upon legislative lawmakers, but upon law enforcers as well. Thus, the interaction between lobbyist and administrator is as important as that between lobbyist and legislator. Second, the various boards and commissions are largely isolated from gubernatorial or legislative control. True, the Governor appoints the membership of most, but for terms that exceed his. True, also, the legislature controls the budgetary allocations of many boards and commissions, but it can exercise very little supervision over expenditure. Divided control (between governor and legislature) turns out, in effect, to be no control. Or, more accurately, semiautonomous administrators respond to the interests of vested clienteles with little or no popular democratic control.

## JUDICIAL AUTHORITY IN TEXAS

Gubernatorial and legislative initiative, legislative bargaining, and administrative application of policies do not constitute the whole of the conversion process. The decisions flowing from these three phases are effective only to the extent that Texans obey them. Widespread disobedience of the law would threaten the very existence of the political system. There is little evidence of widespread disobedience in Texas today, but sporadic violations of laws are not uncommon. Of course, the extent of law violation, or crime, in a system is a very crude measure of the degree of acceptance of the legitimacy of system outputs. Nevertheless, taking such a crude indicator, one must assume that Texas is a state where there is at least some instability. In 1965, for example, Texas ranked 18th among the states in crime rates per 10,000 and 8th in its prison population per 10,000 residents.[19]

In some respects law violators articulate demands upon the political system for exemption from the general policies of the state. To determine the legitimacy of those demands, and hence the legitimacy of the laws being violated, a political system must have some institutional procedure for feeding claims into the political system. In state polities the courts are such institutions. In effect, the judiciary processes the claims of citizens against the laws of the state, be they traffic laws, marital and divorce statutes, welfare laws, educational policies, or whatever.

The judicial structure of Texas for organizing the feedback phase of the conversion process is, to say the least, cumbersome. Taken in simplest form, it consists of four levels of courts. At the lowest are justice of the peace and municipal, or corporation, courts; the former process petty cases, both civil and criminal, while the latter process petty criminal cases within cities. At the next higher level are county courts; these may serve as courts of original jurisdiction in civil and criminal cases or hear appeals of cases originating at the lower level. At the third level are district courts, which serve as courts of original jurisdiction in all felonious criminal cases and civil cases involving $1000 or more; 182 district courts existed in Texas at the close of the 1960s. Finally, at the highest level, appeals go to the Court of Criminal Appeals, fourteen Courts of Civil Appeals, and the Supreme Court of Texas. These courts are multiple-member bodies, not single-judge ones as at the lower levels. Complicating this judicial hierarchy are juvenile courts, probate courts, small claims courts, and courts of domestic relations. Thus, as with legislative committees and administrative boards and commissions, there is a proliferation of discretion and responsibility for policies.

---

[19]Thomas R. Dye, *Politics in States and Communities* (Englewood Cliffs, New Jersey: Prentice-Hall, Inc., 1969), pp. 193-94.

Texas is one of 18 states that select judges through nonpartisan election rather than through partisan election, legislative choice, appointment, or a combination thereof. Terms are four years for trial judges, six years for appellate judges. Although district judges and above must be lawyers, this is not necessary below the district level. But, the nonpartisan election arrangement for judicial selection should not be taken at face value. In actuality, both the Governor and county commissions have authority to fill vacancies in the judiciary; in practice, they do so with relative frequency. Once appointed, judges rarely are opposed in reelection bids and rarely defeated when opposed.[20]

The effectiveness of the judiciary in processing feedbacks depends upon the access people have to it as well as upon its structure and the selection of judicial officials. The impoverished and ignored Texan—black, white, and Mexican-American—hesitates to press demands in court for lack of funds. These impoverished interests are involved in criminal cases with high frequency; it is questionable—given the heavy case load of the courts, the fact that lower court judges need not have legal backgrounds, and the fact that judicial selection is based upon an appointive-nonpartisan election scheme in which the poor rarely vote—that the treatment they receive in this phase of policy conversion is equivalent to that obtained by the more affluent interests.

# THE FRAGMENTED ORGANIZATION OF THE TEXAS CONVERSION PROCESS

We may conclude this discussion of policy-making institutions in the Texas political system by reiterating a theme that emerged from our consideration of the governing structure provided by the Constitution of 1876. Although that document speaks of the coordination of governing powers by three separate, autonomous, and unified departments—executive, legislative, and judicial—we have found that the realities are different. As converters of social inputs into policy outputs in the Texas political system, these institutions are characterized by internal proliferation of discretionary units, overlapping functions, competing loyalties, absence of centralized planning, and privileged access for established interests at the expense of the ignored.

---

[20]Bancroft C. Henderson and T. C. Sinclair, "The Selection of Judges in Texas," *Houston Law Review*, 5 (January 1968), 430, and *The Selection of Judges in Texas* (Houston: Public Affairs Research Center, University of Houston, 1965), pp. 17-32.

Without question this fragmented, or pluralist, organization of the Texas conversion process has a determining effect upon the types of policy outputs of which the political system is capable. Each demand, stress, or strain from the environment must be responded to piecemeal. Each proposed addition to the body of public policy is evaluated not on the basis of its impact upon all Texans, nor on the basis of the consequences it might have for the total political system. Instead, policy considerations focus upon what each proposal might do to one interest or another, one privilege or another, one group or another. Incremental changes in existing policies replace comprehensive reappraisals of the body of public policy, the structure of long-standing priorities, and deficiencies in constitutional structure.[21] As we shall see in the next chapter, in our discussion of the allocation of benefits and burdens, the fragmentation of the conversion process in Texas makes neither reform nor reformation likely in the foreseeable future.

---

[21]See A. J. Thomas, Jr. and Ann Van Wynen Thomas, "The Texas Constitution of 1876," *Texas Law Review*, 35, (October 1957), 907-18. Also, see Howard A. Calkins, "The Need for Constitutional Revision in Texas," *Texas Law Review*, 21 (May 1943), 479-89. O. Douglas Weeks called long ago for a Texas leadership that would free the legislature and the executive from the influence of the lobby. See his article, "The Texas Legislature—A Problem for Constitutional Revision," *Texas Law Review*, 21, (May 1943), 498.

# 6

# Allocating Costs and Benefits

The products of the input and conversion processes in political systems are policy outputs. These may take the form of decisions intended simply to maintain conventional government operations—for instance, the passage of rules of legislative procedure, appointments to the governor's administrative staff, or even resolutions honoring outstanding citizens. But the most significant policy outputs are those that continuously adjust the political system to its changing environment. These outputs arise in response to interest demands and award scarce resources to some groups while depriving others. It is upon these, the outputs that allocate benefits and costs throughout the Texas social system, that we focus our attention in this chapter.[1]

---

[1]There have been attempts to apply a market concept to these allocations of scarce goods and resources and to treat political interests and awards within this market analysis. Those interested in this technique should probably start with Joyce and William Mitchell, *Political Analysis and Public Policy: An Introduction to Political Science* (Chicago: Rand McNally and Co., 1969). Also, see James M. Buchanan and Gordon Tullock, *The Calculus of Consent: Logical Foundations of Constitutional Democracy* (Ann Arbor, Michigan: The University of Michigan Press, 1962); Anthony Downs, *An Economic Theory of Democracy* (New York: Harper and Brothers, 1957); and William H. Riker, *The Theory of Coalitions* (New Haven, Conn.: Yale University Press, 1962).

## VARIETIES OF PUBLIC POLICIES

Political scientists classify the policy outputs of political systems in several ways. In one scheme, for example, policies are labeled as they pertain to social welfare (education, aid to the aged, medical care, public health, etc.), economic concerns (business, labor, agriculture, and the professions), and civil rights. In another, policies are classified according to the branch of government most directly concerned with making them—executive, legislative, or judicial. Useful as these approaches may be, we prefer to think of policy outputs in terms of three varieties—distributive, redistributive, and regulatory.[2]

Distributive policies are those which take relatively abundant natural, social, and economic resources and award them to specific interests. When the American West was settled, for example, the federal government parceled out seemingly inexhaustible tracts of land to farmers, ranchers, railroads, speculators, prospectors, and others opening the frontier. The fact that the resources awarded were not scarce made competition between interests for the government favors unlikely. In Texas there were several sorts of distributive outputs—land grants from Mexico prior to the founding of the Republic, coastal region land for settlement and exploitation, air and streams for the unfettered dumping of industrial waste, and oil, of course, with wildcatters drilling for black gold with little interference from political authorities. But distributive policies recede into the background when resources become scarce and interests no longer can get what they want from the government without competition.

Regulatory policies are those aimed, at least in theory, at assuring that the groups who have obtained awards use those resources in the "public interest" rather than for purely selfish gain. However, the effort to balance private and public claims is difficult, for those not permitted to enjoy the fruits of their resources withdraw their support from elected authorities. Also, the law that benefits one interest adversely affects another. Hence, the tendency is for officials to permit special interests to govern themselves in conjunction with agencies especially created to deal with them; in Texas, for example, the oil industry negotiates its advantages more with the Railroad Commission than with the governor or the legislature. The upshot of regulatory policies is that those interests which established special privileges during periods of distributive output retain them, whereas those on the outside when awards were distributed remain on the outside.

Redistributive policies are directed, as the term suggests, at redistributing the original grants of resources that have since become scarce to the

---

[2]These categories are suggested by Theodore J. Lowi, "American Business, Public Policy, Case-Studies, and Political Theory," *World Politics*, 18 (July 1966), 677-715.

"haves" and "have nots." A principal technique for accomplishing this is to take wealth from some groups through taxation and redistribute it to others by means of welfare, educational, public health assistance, and other policies. In this respect, then, the state budget is a significant tool in allocating benefits and costs through the political system. This is the case in Texas, but is the effect redistributive or regulatory?

## BUDGETARY OUTPUTS: REDISTRIBUTIVE OR REGULATORY?

The best place to examine the struggle over costs and allocation of scarce resources is in the making of the budget. Here the burdens of government are established, relative costs ascertained, and decisions made about which interests are to be rewarded and which are to be cut or sacrificed entirely. Here policy-makers enact the priorities of society. Although the budget represents many things, in its final form it establishes a set of allocated costs and a hierarchy of values.[3]

A regime value (see Chapter 2) common to both state and federal political systems is firm legislative control of the purse in the raising and expenditure of public funds. In the early years of the American republic, popular control of the purse strings exercised by the legislature was viewed as a way of gaining support from the people who bore the cost of maintaining the government, of making the executive dependent upon the legislature, and of reducing arbitrary executive action and rendering the executive accountable.[4] As part of the required procedure, revenue bills could originate only in the lower house. The result of constitutional requirements in all states was a legislative budget, prepared and enacted by the legislature and presented to the governor. Starting as a reform movement in 1899, the National Municipal League championed an executive budget. Twenty-two years later, Congress passed the Budget and Accounting Act of 1921, which required an executive budget at the federal level. Gradually, the states also shifted to an executive budget, and more than 43 states now make the governor or his staff responsible for the preparation of the budget. However, Texas and Nebraska still require both a legislative and an executive budget. In other states where the governor does not have sole control over budget-

---

[3]Aaron Wildavsky, in his *The Politics of the Budgetary Process* (Boston: Little, Brown and Co., 1964), has listed things which the budget represents.

[4]For a concise statement about the history of budgeting from the Magna Carta to the present, see Jesse Burkead, *Government Budgeting* (New York: John Wiley and Sons, Inc., 1956), Chap. I.

making, the budget is the responsibility of a budget commission composed of several state officials—governor, chief budget officer, comptroller, treasurer, attorney general, secretary of state, the commissioner of agriculture, and the superintendent of schools.

The division of legislative and executive responsibility is as follows: In an attempt to bring more order into the budgetary process in Texas, the legislature in 1949 created the Legislative Budget Board (described in Chapter 5). Through its director and staff, the Legislative Budget Board prepares a budget for submission in January of each odd-numbered year. Since 1951 the Governor has been required to submit a budget within five days after the legislature has convened in its regular session. The Executive Budget Office prepares this budget for him.

Both the legislative and executive budgets list the cost of all the agencies (except the cost of the legislature), the amount appropriated in the last biennium, the amount requested by the agencies, and the amount recommended by the Legislative Budget Board and by the Governor. Included in the Legislative Budget Board's document is an estimate from the Comptroller of Public Accounts as to the *expected* revenue available. The Comptroller of Public Accounts is further required by the Constitution to submit an itemized statement of the financial condition of the state. Each legislative house has a committee to hold hearings after the general revenue and appropriation bills are introduced. Revenue measures go to the House Committee on Revenue and Taxation and to the Senate Committee on Finance; appropriation measures go to the House Committee on Appropriations and the Senate State Affairs Committee.

A crucial phase in the budgetary process is the establishment of guidelines for department and agency heads so that they will know how much to request and expect in the way of support from either the Governor or the Legislative Budget Board. Guidelines are given by the legislature after the Legislative Budget Board has studied between sessions programs to be funded by the state. Studies may be requested either by the legislature or the Lieutenant Governor. Only one set of guidelines is permitted by law; hence, there must be coordination between the Governor's budget officers and the Legislative Budget Board. Once a single set of instructions is agreed upon, it is released to the heads of departments and agencies. Using these guidelines, they prepare their financial requests, submit them to the Legislative Budget Board, and await the recommendations of the board's examiner. Final recommendations are made by the board and submitted to the legislature.

It should be noted that it is during the election year (when the legislature is not in session), that both the Governor and the Lieutenant Governor (the latter through the Legislative Budget Board) prepare the budget proposal to be placed before the legislature when it comes into session in January of the following year. This means that the two executive officers, the house members of the Legislative Budget Board, and perhaps even some senate members of the board, prepare the budget proposal while seeking reelection (or, if not seeking reelection, during the last year of their current term in office). This cannot help but color their judgment of agency requests, for they are likely to favor agencies serving interests that must be courted in the reelection campaign.

There are constitutional provisions in Texas which prevent the legislature from manipulating revenues and expenditures freely. Portions of revenue, for example, are earmarked for special funds (the Teacher Retirement Fund and the State Building Fund) and for bond obligations (such as Texas College Student Loan Bonds, the Veteran Land Fund, and similar funds made possible by the issuance of obligation bonds). Similarly, selected revenue rates are established by the Constitution. Finally, statutory designation has produced some two hundred special funds which limit flexibility in appropriation acts. With all these limitations, the proportion of special or earmarked funds was 72 percent of the total funds in Texas in 1965.[5]

## THE ALLOCATION OF BENEFITS

Although each agency may not think its activity the most important in the state, its employees believe it is important enough to succeed and prosper. Over a period of years, agency heads become sufficiently conditioned by failures and successes with the legislature to anticipate the best tactics for advancing their agency's interests. In Texas there has developed a practice of rewarding acquisitive and aggressive agencies,[6] whereas most other states rely more upon the governor's request. The agency in Texas learns that in the rough and tumble game of getting a share of limited resources, it must be aggressive and have its requests in recent years well documented. Thus, although part of the increase in requests in recent years can be traced to inflation, much of it is due to agency acquisitiveness.

Texas agencies request an average of about 28 percent above their current expenditures. The Governor's recommendations have usually been considerably lower—about 82 percent of the agency's request. It appears that the legislature rewards the agency, appropriating an increase of about 17 percent over the agency's current expenditure.[7] The indications are that

---

[5]York Willbern, "Personnel and Money," in *The 50 States and Their Local Governments,* ed. James W. Fesler (New York: Alfred A. Knopf, Inc., 1967), pp. 392-97.
[6]Ira Sharkansky, "Agency Request, Gubernatorial Support and Budget Success in State Legislatures," *American Political Science Review,* LXII (December 1968), 1223.
[7]*Ibid.*

in Texas, as contrasted with other states, the Legislative Budget Board has a preferred position in the budget process, for the legislature tends to accept its recommendations above those of the Governor. The most important factor in determining any given year's budget request is the preceding year's appropriation. How the administrator uses his money during the budgeted years helps determine his appropriation for the coming years. Thus, since the current year's budget will be based largely upon the preceding year's appropriation, it is in the interest of each agency head to get a maximum increase in any budget period and to use the money well. At times, the Governor may take the leadership in asking for an increase of one of the activities of the state, as John Connally did when he was running for reelection. Because of his initiative in the field of higher education, expenditures in that area increased 229 percent between the 1959-1960 and 1967-1968 fiscal years.[8]

In Texas, the allocation of resources for specific programs is fairly consistent. The percentages vary slightly from year to year, but average as follows: education, 45.59 percent; highways, 26.36 percent; public welfare, 14.42 percent; eleemosynary and correctional, 4.29 percent; other costs, 9.34 percent. In comparison with other states, Texas ranks around 40th in recipient payments in six welfare areas;[9] fourth in total highway disbursements; and about fifth in total amount spent on elementary and secondary public schools.[10] Obviously, Texas policy-makers prefer to spend the state's money on highways and education rather than welfare.

Beyond the money allocated to bring adjustment to the changing social and physical environment (highways, public health, institutions for youth, etc), there are appropriations designed to maintain specific elements of the political system itself. In Texas these elements include the judiciary, executive and administrative departments and agencies, and the legislature; to protect their appropriations, there is a Saving Clause in each budget used to validate the remaining parts of the act in case some part should be found unconstitutional. The Governor's office and the Senate each receive about $3,000,000 a year; the House $5,500,000; the Legislative Council $600,000; the State Auditor $1,000,000; the Legislative Budget Board $200,000; and the Legislative Reference Library $100,000. Approximately $10,500,000 is spent by the legislature on maintaining itself. The judiciary received about $7,700,000 for its operations in 1970-1971. The three branches of govern-

---

[8]Council of State Governments, *The Book of the States, 1968-69* (Chicago: Council of State Governments, 1968), p. 299.
[9]Richard E. Dawson and James A. Robinson, "The Politics of Welfare," in *Politics in the American States, A Comparative Analysis*, eds. Herbert Jacob and Kenneth N. Vines (Boston: Little, Brown and Co., 1965), pp. 388-91.
[10]Council of State Governments, *The Book of the States*, pp. 318-19, 289.

ment together received 21,100,000 dollars of the total 2.8 billion spent for 1970. Internal maintenance therefore came to only about .07 percent of the total expenditures.[11]

## THE ALLOCATION OF BURDENS

The state must take many factors into consideration when it decides to tax. As a political system surrounded by other systems and including smaller political subsystems, the state must be aware that its taxation policies will have certain consequences. Roughly, there are these factors to consider: (1) the effect upon the state's economy in and of itself and in relation to other states, (2) the effect on the state's local political systems, and (3) the effect upon the *relationship* between state and local systems. Because there are not easy ways to assess these consequences, taxation policies open up a series of political considerations as many people and interests attempt to influence public decisions about who ought to pay how much.

A taxation policy opens up not only political considerations, but social and economic ones as well; it not only represents a decision about raising revenue, but also reflects a policy designed to produce certain social and economic results. Unlike 35 other states, Texas does not employ a broad-based individual income tax. Instead, by avoiding such a tax, it establishes an economic policy which rewards acquisitiveness, promotes "work" and "saving," and allows individuals to build larger estates. When, unlike 41 other states, it refuses to pass a corporation income tax, it makes clear its intentions to protect corporate wealth and to encourage industries and corporations to move to Texas because of a favorable tax pattern.[12] When such a policy is successful and brings in new industry or encourages local wealth, the economic philosophy which demands this type of governmental action is reinforced. The political demands are thus structured to produce an output from the system favorable to entrenched, more affluent, interests.

Since Texas operates within the federal system as one of many states, its taxation policy is geared to produce the most favorable consequences in relation to the other states. Federalism has an impact upon the economic life of the states, and competition between the states may limit the type of taxation policies selected. For instance, a tax rate in Texas might be the deciding factor in a company's locating a plant there rather than in, say,

---

[11]All of these figures are based on the Committee on Appropriations' Substitute Bill for Senate Bill No. 58, *General Appropriations Bill for the Fiscal Years Ending August 31, 1970-71*, and although some figures were changed in the final appropriation act, these figures are substantially the same.
[12]Council of State Governments, *Book of the States*, pp. 107-8, 204.

Louisiana or Oklahoma. Hence, Texas selects the sales tax (which produces about 8 percent of the total revenue for the state) as a substitute for the less regressive income tax, to ensure the least adverse consequences for the economic life of the state. (A *regressive* tax is one in which the same tax burden falls on all citizens regardless of their ability to pay; a *progressive* tax provides a heavier tax burden for the affluent and a lighter one for low income persons).

Any state is also concerned with the impact of its taxation policy upon its local units of governments. These units have traditionally used the property tax as their chief source of revenue. It is the general practice in Texas to limit the amount of property tax which may be imposed. For example, the Texas Constitution prohibits most hospital districts from imposing a tax exceeding seventy-five cents on $100 valuation. Counties, towns, and cities cannot impose an ad valorem tax exceeding eighty cents per $100 valuation, although the legislature may authorize an additional increase of fifteen cents per $100.

States, however, cannot control their overall fiscal policies as easily as federal political system does. The latter may decide to achieve a given goal by using its fiscal powers of increasing interest rates, reducing expenditures, or increasing taxes. This is not possible for states, which operate as subsystems within the whole. National fiscal policy is determined for them, and the state of Texas has relatively little impact on the national economy if it decides to spend less on education than it did in a previous year or to increase the sales tax. In Texas, the projection of the biennial tax rate has to be undertaken without accurate anticipation of changes in the national economy. As a result, it is possible for the state and federal political systems to pursue opposite goals at the same time. For instance, during depressions the federal government might use its powers to stimulate investment while state and local units are reducing their investments (vis-à-vis buildings, highways, etc.). Such contradictions may also exist within the state itself, as, for instance, when Texas stimulates tourism but imposes a hotel-motel tax in hope of passing the tax on to persons and groups coming from outside the state.

An analysis of where Texas derives its revenue shows that the state has chosen to get almost one-third of it from three sources—the sales tax, the highway motor fuel tax, and a gross receipts and productions tax. Each of these produces about 12 percent of the state's revenue. Auto sales tax and license charges produce 8 percent, while tobacco, cigarette, and alcoholic beverage taxes together produce another 8 percent. A tax on franchise fees and permit charges, and an insurance company tax, together produce about 10 percent. Ad valorem taxes, revenue from sales, rentals, and royalties, and revenue from interest and dividends, together produce another

10 percent. The remainder comes from the federal government in the form of grants-in-aid and from local governments.[13]

Texas has traditionally been classified as a low-tax state. Indeed, it is in the lowest quartile of states according to per capita state and local taxes from 1902 until 1962. Its tax rates remain stable from year to year; sudden jumps from a low rate to a high rate are unlikely.[14] Texas has thus established its spending and revenue patterns, and it will probably take some major change in the state's economic or social system to alter them.

A recent innovation in the budget practice in some states has produced many adherents as well as detractors. Borrowing from the Department of Defense, these states have begun to use the program planning budget system (PPBS). Departing from the incremental nature of process budgeting, which has been the usual budgeting method of governments, PPBS stresses the output and its ramifications. The accent is placed not upon the activity itself, but upon what *results* the activity produces. Whereas the traditional bargaining between groups and interests produces a budget that gives little attention to the results produced between groups and the consequences for the entire social structure, program budgeters pride themselves on their ability to analyze and anticipate interactions between subsystems.[15] Advocates believe that by using PPBS they will be better able to relate the consequences of governmental budgeting to all social problems. They point out that the results of alternative inputs and their attendant costs will be weighed against each other in order to arrive at a decision about what to spend and where.

However, there are some who feel that the new budgeting process may have serious drawbacks. They believe that the combination of an improperly trained budget staff and a legislative body which has not been properly introduced to the method may mean serious legislative opposition. They also feel that political decisions represent more than one goal, and that PPBS may not predict adequately with regard to all goals. Further, since goals are another way of referring to values, they also fear that use of the PPBS might transfer basic policy decisions from the legislature to the staff.[16]

---

[13]See the *Report of the Comptroller of Public Accounts, State of Texas, 1968* (Austin, Texas: Comptroller of Public Accounts) for a further breakdown of revenue.

[14]Clara Penniman, "The Politics of Taxation," *Politics in the American States,* eds. Jacob and Vines, pp. 296-97, 314.

[15]See Allen Schick, "Systems Politics and Systems Budgeting," *Public Administration Review*, XXIX, (March-April 1969), 137-51, for a discussion of the merits of systems budgeting over the pluralistic process of incrementalism; see also Bertram M. Gross, "The New Systems Budgeting," *Ibid.*, pp. 113-37.

[16]Frederick C. Mosher, "Limitations and Problems of PPBS in the States," *Public Administration Review,* XXIX (March-April 1969), 160-64.

Two matters are really at issue in this debate over budgetary methods, and both are related to important questions we have discussed previously. First, to the extent that an administrative staff (whether of the legislature or the Governor) made up of technical planning experts decides upon allocations, crucial phases of the conversion process are removed from the hands of elected officials and centralized in the offices of technicians. As we have seen, in Texas there are long-standing tendencies to fragment, not centralize, conversion control. Second, PPBS envisions the budgetary process as a redistributive, not a regulatory, tool. From what we have said about budget-making in Texas, it should be clear now that budgetary outputs have not been redistributive. Many factors lend themselves to a regulatory budgeting scheme in the state—the bestowal of awards primarily to acquisitive agencies on the basis of previous years' appropriations; the control of budget proposals by officials seeking reelection; the direction of priorities toward deemphasizing education, welfare, health, and related spending; and the absence of any truly redistributive tax arrangement such as graduated individual and corporate income taxes. A comprehensive PPBS approach would thus fly in the face of two traditional features of the Texas political system, a fragmented conversion process and a regulatory rather than redistributive output process. Hence, it is with considerable interest that students of Texas politics should look at the consequences of the preparations made in Texas in 1970 to introduce, even on a very limited basis, the PPBS method of budget analysis.

## ECONOMIC OUTPUTS: FURTHER REGULATORY ALLOCATIONS

The regulation of economic activities in Texas is similar to the allocation of resources in that it involves costs within the political system. When policy-makers act with respect to any area of the economy, they recognize that there are dangers of alienating some interests in order to improve the positions of others; by the same token, they are aware that inaction assists some interests while disadvantaging others. Hence, economic regulation is undertaken with the object of optimizing the positions of all major interests as well as those of the policy-makers themselves. No established and influential group gets all it wants, but neither does it come away with nothing or even suffer any great loss. The regulatory process is thus a delicate art of balancing the interests of all whose support is essential for the politician's continuance in office. However, it is an art practiced within a social and cultural environment that influences the types of bargains policy-makers may strike. Certain goals must be elevated and certain behavior praised. Allocations made through the regulation of economic activities must be rationalized in the name of "higher" community values. The regulation of labor and business in the state is a good example.

The history of Texas is one of high expectations. From its settlement until its industrialization, the vastness of its lands held promise to the lowest dirt farmer. It was a state for the impresario. Those who had no high hopes of going beyond their current status did not come. Texas, like many other states, was settled by "boomers," by people who "talked up" the situation. The industrialization of Texas fed this sentiment. Opportunities in oil and business began to rival those in land. The Protestant Ethic became a part of the value system. Work, diligence, and saving became part of the creed. Financial responsibility was internalized as one of the regime values in the Constitution when the amount of the state's allowed indebtedness was limited to two hundred thousand dollars. The Constitution of Texas reads that "No debt shall be created by or on behalf of the State, except to supply casual deficiencies of revenue, repel invasion, suppress insurrection, defend the State in war, or pay existing debt; and the debt created to supply deficiencies in revenue shall never exceed in the aggregate at any one time two hundred thousand dollars."[17] In addition, the Constitution required the Comptroller of Public Accounts to certify always that the anticipated funds in the state treasury would be sufficient to cover an appropriation made by the legislature.

In this milieu, where work was regarded as sacred and indebtedness as a sin, workers achieved the right to organize in 1899.[18] At that time, organized labor consisted largely of craft unions, such as those of the plumbers, carpenters, and bricklayers. But once Texas began to industrialize, it was the unskilled and poorly paid industrial workers, not the stalwart and self-reliant craftsmen, who started making demands—demands that industrialists regarded as threatening to established commercial interests. The legislature responded with laws deterrent to organized labor, although it never repealed the right to organize. In 1943, the legislature passed a bill forbidding a labor organizer to talk to laborers before he had secured a license from the Secretary of State. This act was later declared to be an unconstitutional encroachment upon the freedom of speech,[19] but attempts until then to enforce it had a deterrent effect upon labor's right to organize. Other acts limited the right of assembly by forbidding more than two pickets

---

[17]The Constitution of The State of Texas, Article III, Sections 49 and 49A. Because of the first limitation, the Constitution has been amended to allow the offering of bonds; bonded indebtedness, not being limited by the constitutional stipulation, may exceed the $200,000 limit by any amount.

[18]Article 5152, *Vernon's Texas Statutes* (Kansas City, Mo.: Vernon Law Book Company, 1948).

[19]*Thomas v. Collins*, 323 U. S. 516 (1945).

at any entrance. The Texas Legislature ultimately passed a "right to work" law forbidding "employment on account of membership or nonmembership in a labor union,"[20] and it declared any law which required or prescribed union membership as a condition of employment to be null and void and against public policy. By and large, the impact of such legislation favored business and individual contracting over the labor unions and group contracting. Thus, just as work was assigned a high value, so wealth and property—the fruits of work—were highly prized; in protection of the individual, each person was given the right to sell his labor on the open market at any price he could get or the employer was willing to pay, but in protection of the established interests, minimum wage laws did not become part of the Texas regulation of labor until 1969.

Another way to approach the value of work and the use of laws to encourage work in Texas is to examine the amount of money the state spends on welfare as compared with other states. Texas has generally let the federal government contribute most of the money for this purpose. Federal funds make up about 70 percent of the total, state funds a little more than 27 percent, and local government contributions less than 2 percent. In per capita expenditures for welfare programs, Texas spends only $5.60, thus ranking 42nd among the states.[21] This small amount of expenditure is based upon the premise (questionable) that welfare payments reward indolence and penalize industry. In another move stressing work rather than state aid, Texas has passed legislation which enables the blind to work by giving them the right to operate vending stands on state property. Thus, work is assigned a high value in Texas, particularly when the alternative is state expense.

Another facet of the economic and social values of the state is the importance placed upon competition. Through limitations on monopolies or trusts, much like the antitrust laws of the United States, Texas has attempted to enforce competition artificially. Codes prohibit utilities which do business in two or more towns from engaging in injurious competition; this allows a city to maintain and operate its own utility on a competitive basis. A chain store tax requires each person, group, agent, or store to secure a license from the Comptroller of Public Accounts. Branch banking has been forbidden, in an attempt to promote competition and decentralize financial control. As early as 1909, Texas passed legislation which encouraged local insurance companies by requiring that a company invest in Texas securities a "sum of money equal to at least seventy-five percent of the aggregate amount of the legal reserve required by the laws of the State of its domicile." This law promoted the withdrawal of out-of-state insurance companies and, consequently, the growth of Texas-based companies.

---

[20]Article 5207A, Section 2, *Vernon's Texas Statutes*.
[21]Richard E. Dawson and James A. Robinson, "The Politics of Welfare," pp. 382-93.

The laws also specify that no one company can provide both life and casualty insurance. Laws regulating insurance companies are executed by the Board of Insurance. In addition, there are regulations pertaining to saving and loan associations and banks; these are executed by the State Banking Board and the Banking Department. With all three regulatory agencies, the securing of a charter and license is critical.

Licensing is itself a regulatory device to accomplish several ends: it produces some revenue from the charge or fee of the license; it may be used for the purpose of insuring quality in the profession (e.g., the medical license); it may also be used as a method of policing morals and health (e.g., the pharmaceutical license); or it may be used for the purpose of imposing administrative control (such as the license required for anyone entering a mercantile enterprise of any sort, which facilitates the collection of the sales tax). Unfortunately, no attempt has been made to do a thorough study of what impact the 25 professional examining and licensing boards of Texas have upon the state's economy or upon a single profession.

The Railroad Commission, established in 1891 and gradually granted wider and wider jurisdiction, is perhaps the most important regulatory commission in Texas, regulating the railroad, trucking, bus, and oil industries. Since the oil wars and near collapse of the oil producers and distributors in the 1930s, the primary function of the commission is now called "conservation." This involves regulating the number and spacing of wells for production and determining how much may be pumped in any given month. The result is not only conservation but the maintenance of an artificial price for the oil by making it scarce. The costs involved in eliminating this by-product of conservation, however, would be high indeed, for it would force the Texas oil industry to compete in the federal system against states which also set prices as an indirect consequence of conservation.

# REACTION TO POLICY-MAKING: SUPPORT, OPPOSITION, OR ACQUIESCENCE?

As we have seen, the age of distributive outputs is largely over in Texas and the imbalance between redistributive and regulatory outputs indicates that Texans now live in the age of the regulatory state. There is no evidence to suggest that the vast majority of Texans are dissatisfied with such an arrangement. Indeed, the state grows and prospers. According to estimates of the U. S. Bureau of the Census population research center, Texas' population increased in the decade of the 1960s by 14.7 percent—more rapid a growth than in the United States as a whole or in states of a similar population size in 1960. A substantial portion of the increase reflects the fact that more people have been moving into the state than out of it.[22] Commerce, industry, business, labor, and agriculture also made marked gains in the 1960s. We suspect that the romanticized self-image of Texas prospers as well; "The Yellow Rose of Texas" is being sung as lustily in the 1970s as it was in the decade before.[23]

Nor can we say that the Texas regime or its authorities are under serious challenge. Constitutional revision is much discussed, but little action is taken. In the face of rising difficulties resulting from long-term budget planning, Texans stick doggedly to the biennial budget. In the face of difficulties produced by short executive terms and rising campaign costs, Texans reject constitutional amendments for longer, four-year, gubernatorial terms. And although Texans in various minority groups find political participation less restricted to them and somewhat more rewarding because of repeal of the poll tax and legislative reapportionment, it must be recalled that these were regime changes stimulated by federal court decisions rather than by established state interests. Texans are ambivalent about further extension of the franchise. A 1970 Texas Poll revealed that 48 percent of Texans favored lowering the voting age to 18 years, 49 percent favored leaving it at 21 years, and 3 percent were undecided (at a period when a nationwide Gallup Poll revealed that 58 percent of American adults surveyed favored lowering the required voting age).[24]

Finally, what of the response of Texans to specific policy outputs? Unfortunately, there is little available evidence bearing on this question. What data exist present a mixed and unclear picture. Polls, for example, indicate that Texans in early 1970 were not satisfied with Texas liquor laws (67 percent said they favored local option elections to determine whether liquor should be sold by the drink),[25] and 63 percent of Texans surveyed in 1970 favored easing Texas laws pertaining to abortion.[26] Yet Texans prefer more restrictive approaches in other matters. In 1969, for instance, 62 percent of those surveyed urged new laws placing even "tougher penalties" on

---

[22]"Texas Population Rises 'Moderately,'" *The Dallas Morning News,* March 12, 1970.

[23]Legend has it that this now famous song was actually written about Emily Morgan, a mulatto slave girl (referred to as a "high yaller gal" in the language of the time). Emily, it seems, may have turned the course of Texas history: As all Texans learn very early, the war for Texas independence came to a successful climax with the defeat of the forces of Mexican General Santa Anna at the Battle of San Jacinto on April 21, 1836. Santa Anna stumbled so slowly from his tent that he was late for the battle with the attacking forces of Sam Houston; mythology records, even if history does not, that he preferred Emily in the tent to the Texans outside. *See* David Nevin, *The Texans* (New York: William Morrow & Company, Inc., 1968), pp. 62-63.

[24]"The Texas Poll," *The Dallas Morning News,* May 3, 1970.

[25]"The Texas Poll," *The Dallas Morning News,* May 17, 1970.

[26]"The Texas Poll," *The Dallas Morning News,* July 19, 1970.

the sale and use of marijuana,[27] and in the controversial area of student demonstrations on Texas college campuses, 79 percent of those polled in 1970 believed the National Guard should take a firm hand in quelling disturbances (71 percent approved of the use of loaded guns by troops).[28]

It would be a mistake to assume from such poll results that all Texans are vitally concerned about political issues. Rather, it is more accurate to say that on most issues, whether they are before Texas officials for decision or merely publicized in the news media, Texans are little informed and little concerned. They probably neither support existing legislation nor oppose it, neither support proposed changes nor oppose them. The vast majority of Texans silently accept the established body of law, acquiescing to its formulation, passage, and enforcement.

Texas laws receive the acquiescence of Texans, by and large, in keeping with the general ideological context of the society. If our analysis is credible, the regime values and regime norms are embodied in the outputs of the political system. The tax structure and the allocation of benefits are products of a deeply held faith in the value of work. The sales tax, the absence of the income tax, the anti-union legislation, and the right to work law all reflect an abiding faith in work. In fact, the right *to* work law is really a right *of* work law. The allocation processes protect work and its rights of reward. Wealth, avidly sought as the end of work, becomes a right just as work has been a right. Both have been legitimized within the Texas political system. Only recently has pressure of a different variety emerged. The poor and the uneducated, the blacks and the browns, are making qualitatively different demands upon the system. And, just as the system stability is fostered by the support of the benefited and acquiescence of the "silent majority," so a system change may yet be the result of the growing self-awareness of these emerging minorities.

---

[27]"The Texas Poll," *The Dallas Morning News*, November 11, 1969.
[28]"The Texas Poll," *The Dallas Morning News, July 12, 1970.*

# A POSTSCRIPT

*PART FOUR*

# 7

# System Stability and Change

As we complete our description and interpretation of the workings of the Texas political system, this is an appropriate point to summarize our major themes, look forward to the future of Texas politics, and evaluate the nature of Texas democracy. In the process, we will again employ a major postulate of systems analysis—the ever-changing relationship of the polity to its environmental surroundings.

## SUMMARY ASPECTS OF TEXAS POLITICS

We said at the outset that a political system is a set of human interactions that take place in a social, economic, constitutional, and cultural environment and function to regulate disputes over the allocation of values in society. The polity, we noted, converts a continuing flow of inputs (supports and demands) from the environment into policy outputs (benefits and deprivations). Using this model of political activity, we have described in turn the environments, demands, supports, conversions, and outputs of the Texas political system.

Of the several politically relevant aspects of the Texas environment, a few are particularly noteworthy. Socially, Texas is a diverse state comprising three major ethnic groups—white Texans, black Texans, and Mexican-American Texans—distributed in several changing, but still reasonably distinct, regions. The Texas economy is rapidly developing and modernizing, comparing well in that respect with other states. But not all Texans benefit equally from the economic environment, and Texas emerges as a state with wide gaps between the affluent and the poor. For example, the lowest income-earners receive a smaller proportion of the state's aggregate income than their proportion among all income-earners; conversely, the highest income-earners receive a portion far in excess of their relative numbers in that population. Ranking all 50 state on the basis of the unequal distribution of incomes among their residents, Texas emerges as the 11th highest in income inequality (states such as Mississippi, Arkansas, Alabama, and Tennessee have the most unequal income distributions).[1]

Social diversity and economic disparities have not, however, been serious threats to the constitutional arrangement in Texas for almost a century. The long-established political community and the constituted regime embodying its values have both been relatively stable as political systems go. The fragmentation of the authority structure—implied in the operating principles of separated powers, checks and balances, and interest representation—was revered in the 1800s and is apparently beyond serious modification even today.

The pattern of political supports arising from this environment, although not unique to Texas, is clearly Texan in tone and content. A basically traditionalistic political culture supports a social order generated in less than a century by the adroit exploitation of open country, oil resources, and modern technology. Resting comfortably alongside this traditionalistic orientation is an individualistic one that minimizes the role of government authorities in stimulating social change or regulating economic affairs. The combined traditionalistic-individualistic elements are exhibited in limited partisan competition and in the citizens' markedly low levels of political participation, seen in a general context of mass indifference.

This pattern of supports colors the presentation of demands. In Texas, organized pressure groups lobby on behalf of discrete, established interests. The pluralist elite remains exclusive, its exclusiveness perpetuated by the acquiescence of the middle class and the simple lack of resources and organization of the impoverished.

We have suggested that the input pattern results in a conversion process largely under the operation and control of relatively few interests. The social conflicts regulated by formal authorities are those of established interests disagreeing among themselves as to who shall be rewarded and who shall pay the costs of preserving the social order. Inter-institutional conflicts (between the Governor and the Senate, say, as in the Connally era, or

---

[1]Thomas R. Dye, "Income Inequality and American State Politics," *American Political Science Review*, LXIII (March 1969), 157-62.

between the legislature and the Land Commissioner as in the Smith era) may have little to do with the more poorly articulated, but nonetheless basic, demands of the Texas minorities—be they ethnic groups, taxpayers, consumers, urban dwellers, or whatever. As a result, the process of conversion as it operated in the Texas political system in the 1960s passed on a legacy of social problems unresolved by appropriate policy outputs.

What are the critical areas of social dispute before the Texas political authorities now, in the 1970s? They are numerous. One is certainly education. Here the problem is multifold, touching upon questions of academic excellence, vocational and technical education, teachers' salaries, curriculum improvement, funding for new facilities, equalization of school taxes, etc. From the perspective of interest representation, however, two questions are particularly pertinent. First, what is the purpose of public education in Texas? In the 1960s the rationale for increased funding in education was a simple one—to provide an educational environment in Texas that would retain the state's talented youth rather than permit a "brain drain" to other states. The result, so it seemed, would be a large pool of professional and skilled personnel from which established economic interests in Texas could draw sustenance. But education for the benefit of an exclusive interest falls short of the normal meaning of the "public education" concept. In the 1970s the decision must be made as to whether the clientele ultimately served by educational policy is to be broadened or whether educational policy is, in the traditionalistic pattern, to benefit the established social order.

Second, there is the related question of equality of educational opportunity for all Texans. A study by the Department of Health, Education, and Welfare indicates that at the close of the 1960s—sixteen years after segregation policies became unconstitutional—63.1 percent of all Texas' black students were still isolated in schools which were 95 to 100 percent black.[2] One-fourth of all Texas' black students attended schools still predominantly black. Moreover, 72.3 percent of all Mexican-American students in Texas attended schools where their minority comprised the majority of students. In the face of continuing pressures (inputs) from the federal system, Texas must resolve its problems of educational opportunity in the current decade.

Educational outputs, however, depend upon financing, another major area of social dispute. Policies dealing with urban areas (air pollution, transportation, etc.), welfare, mental health, water supply and pollution, and sundry other concerns also require adequate financing. There is a demand now in Texas for new areas from which to raise money, and this implies a concern about what interests are to pay higher taxes—be they income taxes, sales

---

[2]See "Desegregation Report," *Congressional Quarterly*, XXVIII (January 9, 1970), 124-25.

taxes, corporate taxes, excises, or whatever. In short, the input-output process in Texas, as elsewhere, carries with it the potential of redistributing the wealth and resources of citizens. But who will control that conversion? The answer will depend upon quiet changes taking place in the environment of the Texas political system.

## IMPLICATIONS OF SYSTEM CHANGES

In any political system people frequently remain quiescent when, to the outsider, the conditions of their existence warrant their demanding improvements. The reason is that "mass behavior is linked more directly to socially cued beliefs and perceptions than to empirically manifest conditions."[3] A citizenry tends to symbolize its hopes and fears, aspirations and expectations, not on the basis of objective realities but in accordance with illusions that are far more satisfying to accept. To the extent that the environments and structures of a political system appear to conform to widely accepted symbols, the supports and demands of various interests do not overload the capacity of the polity to respond. Those rewarded by the system continue to be rewarded, those deprived continue to be deprived, and those feeling that they are unaffected continue to acquiesce. But should changes occur in either the environment or structure of the political system, a new pattern of supports and demands may emerge.

An argument in vogue among some political scientists is that "differences in policy, at least in certain substantive areas, are more readily explained in terms of differences in the socioeconomic environments of the states than by the examination of structural variables."[4] To the extent that this is correct, changes in socioeconomic factors may herald significant shifts in policy. In Texas, such socioeconomic transformations are developing. In population growth alone, the changes are impressive. The estimated 1970 population of Texas is 11.7 million, an increase of well over 2 million in the last decade. And increasing numbers imply increasing demands for all types of goods and services.

Outputs in the area of education, alluded to previously, will certainly be affected by these population shifts. The number of Texans between 15 and 24 years of age will be over 2 million in the 1970s, half again as large as in the 1960s. Neither high schools nor colleges can meet such increases without turning to political avenues for added resources. At the other end

---

[3] Murray Edelman, "Escalation and Ritualization of Political Conflict," *American Behavioral Scientist,* 13 (November-December 1969), 231.

[4] Richard I. Hofferbert, "The Relation Between Public Policy and Some Structural and Environmental Variables in the American States," *American Political Science Review,* LX (March 1966), 73.

of the age spectrum, the numbers of persons 65 years of age and over will have increased from 728,000 in 1960 to well over 1 million in the 1970s. The resulting need for well-developed welfare programs for the aged will inject demands never before faced by Texas authorities on such a broad scale. In fact, the rising proportion of persons in the "dependent ages" (under 15, and 65 or over) suggests the emergence of newly articulate interests in the near future.

The increasing militancy of Texas blacks and Mexican-Americans, slowly made evident in the late 1960s, will be accompanied by increasing numbers in these ethnic groups in the 1970s. The nonwhite population alone will exceed 1.5 million in this decade, suggesting a growing constituency for minority leaders of all persuasions bent on changing established patterns of political supports and demands.

Finally, the shifts in population that have already occurred in the 1970s imply the continued expansion of metropolitan Texas. In the 1970s more than 80 percent of Texans will live in urban areas and 70 percent in metropolitan areas. Problems of furnishing housing, transportation, pollution control, welfare payments, and health and educational facilities will multiply in ways never dreamed of by the few men who designed the 1876 Constitution.[5]

But the Texas political system will be responding to structural as well as socioeconomic changes in the current decade, and this will make the 1876 Constitution seem even less relevant to environmental stresses than in the past. Many of the structural changes will take place in informal practices and customs rather than in formal and fundamental laws. For instance, while it is unlikely that the one-party character of Texas politics running from "court house to state house" will be replaced by effective two-party competition in the near future, it is apparent that the Republican party now has more than a mere beachhead. The migration into Texas of Republicans, the socialization of younger Texans in Republican loyalties, and the few but important conversions of lifelong Democrats provide a basis for a more competitive minority party than heretofore experienced in Texas. And within the Democratic party, the growth of minority constituencies among the black, young, urban, and Mexican-American Texans holds promise for a more competitive, intraparty, factional rivalry (made even more competitive by internal party reforms on both the national and state levels).

It seems likely that the redistricting of the state legislature on the basis of the 1970 census will produce, for the first time in Texas, a House of Representatives and a Senate in which urban areas have dominant representation. Dramatic shifts in policy outputs are unlikely, yet the tone and tenor

---

[5]Stanley A. Arbingast, "Some Comments on the Preliminary 1970 Census Data," *Texas Business Review*, XLIV (July 1970), 178-79.

of legislative politics will gradually evolve in directions not easily recognized by Texans of earlier decades. For one thing, the agenda of politics—the types of problems debated—will undoubtedly focus upon the demands and resources characteristic of a technological society.

Nevertheless, in the midst of a growing and shifting population, economic development along technological lines, and partisan and districting changes in structure, there will remain much stability in the Texas political system. Constitutional revisions of major proportion remain unlikely. The protected privileges of established interests, sewn firmly into the fabric of present administrative institutions, will remain to insulate many political authorities from popular control. Indeed, the alterations in Texas government, if they follow the pattern of the past, will imply a future very much like the past. In Texas, the way the political system has traditionally adjusted to changes in the environment has been for political authorities to reward newly emergent—hence demanding—interests with preferred policy outputs in exchange for active support. It is easy to foresee that the future transactions of the polity with its environment will be much the same. In short, representation will be extended to the more vocal minorities to the degree that they become their own governors, making policies on their own behalf. It is unlikely that they will have coequal status with the insurance industry, oil producers, manufacturers, ranchers, and other established interests, yet they will probably receive a long-awaited "piece of the action." What of the character of the republic—the representative democracy—should this occur?

## THE PATTERNS OF TEXAS DEMOCRACY

It will be recalled that in Chapter 1 we outlined three patterns of democracy characteristic of modern political systems. *Participatory* democracy, we said, implies the full and continuous participation of highly motivated, informed, and rational citizens with access to policy-making centers; *pluralist* democracy implies indirect influence over policy-making by citizens through their membership in special-interest groups; and *elitist* democracy implies a system in which an oligarchy rules largely in the interests of its own members but in the name of the mass. From what we have said throughout this work, it should be apparent that the Texas political system possesses characteristics of each of these patterns. It formally provides the minimal institutions of a participatory democracy (popular elections, free speech and press, free assembly, etc.); it embraces the pressure organizations of a pluralist democracy; and it is dominated in policy-making by the established interests of an elitist democracy.

At several points we have alluded to this hybrid pattern as that of a pluralist elite, composed basically of organized established interests competing with one another not only in legislative matters but even before the citizenry in elections through the dominant Democratic party. If this is a fair appraisal of the democratic pattern in Texas today, what *speculations* can we offer about its character in the coming years of the 1970s? First, it seems clear that widespread participation of Texans in policy-making will remain primarily symbolic for several years to come. Relatively few Texans will take an active interest in the social conditions that give rise to political controversies, and few will seek to understand these controversies, let alone participate in their resolution. In short, participation will be characterized as much by acquiescence to policy outputs as by the active shaping of them.

Second, however, to the extent that pluralist democracy depends upon the organization and representation of interests, we may expect an increase in the pluralist dimension of Texas politics. Minorities on all sides—black and white, urban and rural, young and old, prosperous and deprived—will articulate demands through pressure organizations. Hence, if we had a way of measuring the support and demand levels of a political system, we might see the levels of symbolic support in Texas politics remaining fairly stable, but with a marked increase in the level of conflicting organized demands.

Finally, as suggested above, through structural changes the pluralist elite that traditionally has controlled the conversion process in Texas politics will expand. With expansion will come diversification as newly emergent interests are granted secure positions and protected privileges in the Texas oligarchy; in the process, intra-elite competition will increase and be carried more frequently into the public forum, perhaps as election rituals waged through a slowly increasing competitive party system.

But a pluralist elite is still an elite. Whether or not its rule qualifies as democratic depends not upon any intrinsic meaning of democracy itself but upon the satisfactions derived by both the elite and mass of the population in their continuing interactions. Proponents of participatory democracy cannot help but wince at the prospect, but in the foreseeable future the community and regime values of the Texas polity will remain essentially unchanged as the political system responds to stresses from its vastly changing environments.

# Index

Abernethy, Byron R., 111n
Access
  defined, 92-93
  tactics, 99
Administrative agencies
  authority, 128-29
  in conversion process, 14
  number, 129
  and political outputs, 13
Adrian, Charles R., 36n, 48n
Advisory Committee, 34
Age
  and poverty, 89
  and voting requirements, 66
Agriculture, decline in Texas, 27-28
Allen, Ruth A., 48n
Allocations
  of benefits, 137-39
  of burdens, 139-42
  in political system, 5
Almond, Gabriel A., 9n, 75n, 117n
American Federation of Labor-Congress of Industrial Organization (AFL-CIO), 29, 30n, 84, 96, 102
American Legion, 83
Anglos, as Texas population grouping, 20, 25
Arbingast, Stanley A., 22n, 25n, 153n
Association for the Protection of German Immigrants in Texas, 26

Attorney General, Texas, 108, 111, 129
Austin, Moses, 25

Baer, Michael, 97n, 98n, 122n
Banking Department, 145
Barber, James David, 122n, 123n
Bargaining, in conversion process, 14, 126-27
Barnes, Ben, 114, 121, 125
Beale, Calvin L., 48n
Belden, Joe, 116. *See also* The Texas Poll
Bell, Wendell, 70n
Beyle, Thad L., 112n
Black Texans, 20, 25-26, 149
  and judicial treatment, 131
  militancy, 153
  and political parties, 58, 65
  poverty, 86-92
  and voting rates, 68
Boards and commissions, types and conversion roles, 128-29
Board of Insurance, 145
Bogue, Donald J., 48n
Bonine, Michael E., 22n, 25n
Bonjean, Charles M., 58n
Boskoff, Alvin, 69n
Boundaries, of political systems, 7-8
Browning, Harley L., 22n
Buchanan, James M., 133n
Buchanan, William, 102n, 122n

## Index 161

Buckley, Walter, 2n
Budget and Accounting Act, 135
Budgetary processes, 133-47
  executive, 135
  guidelines, 136
  PPBS, 141-42
  program allocations, 138
  redistributive vs. regulatory, 135-42
Burdine, J. Alton, 112n
Burkhead, Jesse, 135n
Bush, George, 73
*Bush* v. *Martin*, 40n

Calkins, Howard A., 132n
Campaigns, electoral
  candidates information, 117
  costs, 95-96
  and institutionalized privilege, 95-96
  and interest groups, 95-97
  regulating expenditures, 96
  versus policy, 95
Campbell, Angus, 69n
Carl, Prince of Solms-Braunfels, 26
Carr, Waggoner, 121
Central Texas, as a region, 47
Chambers, William Trout, 29n
Cherry, H. Dicken, 125, 125n, 127n
Civil War, in Texas, 25, 26, 33
Clark, Ed, 115
Clark, Lee, 83n, 100n, 102n
Cnudde, Charles F., 27n
Coleman, James S., 117n
Collins-Knagg, 96
Commissioner of the General Land Office, Texas, 108
Committee on Appropriations, Texas House of Representatives, 136
Committee on Finance, Texas Senate, 136
Committee on Revenue and Taxation, Texas House of Representatives, 136
Committee system, in Texas Legislature, 121
  conference committees, 126-27
  discretion, 125
Community power structures, 84
Comparative analysis, 2-14, 27
Comptroller of Public Accounts, Texas, 108, 113, 129, 136, 143
Conflict resolution, as requisite of social system, 4
Connally, John, 109, 114, 115, 116, 117, 118, 138
Conservatism, Texas, 28, 30
Constitutional environment
  of political systems, 8
  protection of privilege, 93-95
  rules of fragmentation, restriction, and representation, 9
  of Texas, 33-42
Constitution of 1876, 35-36
  amendment process, 38
  and conflict-of-interest, 120
  and conversion process, 108
  and economic regulation, 143
  and fragmentation of authority, 131-32
  and governorship, 118
  and political roles, 108-9
  and protection of privilege, 94-95
  restrictive regime values, 38
  revision, 35-36
  special fund allocations, 137
  support for, 45-46
  and Texas Legislature, 37, 120
Constitutions of Texas, 35
Consultation of the Chosen Delegates of All Texas, 34
Converse, Philip E., 69n
Conversion process, 6, 8, 13-14, 45, 133, 149, 150-51
  control, 142
  fragmentation, 131-32
  legislative, 123-28
  phases of initiation, bargaining, application, and feedback, 14, 108
  structure and roles, 107-32
Correlation analysis, 69-72
Corwin, Edward S., 15n
Council of State Governments, 138n, 139
County courts, 130
Court of Criminal Appeals, 130
Courts of Civil Appeals, 130
Cowart, Andrew T., 92n
Crime, Texas rates, 130
Crittenden, John, 10n, 31n, 32n
Cultural environment, of Texas political system, 9, 46-54

Daniel, Price, 115
Davis, J. William, 36n, 121n
Dawson, Irving Owen, 35n, 104n, 109n
Dawson, Richard E., 138n, 144n
Demands, political
  campaigning, 95-97
  institutionalizing privilege, 93-95
  lobbying, 97-103
  as political inputs, 10-11, 150
  techniques of presenting, 92-103
Democracies, types, 15-17, 154
Democratic party, Texas, 35, 40, 56, 153
  and agriculture, 28
  elitist rule, 155
  fragmentation, 61
  and governorship, 116
  identifiers, 58

## Index

and ideology, 64
as mobilizer of supports, 61
Democrats
  conservative, 64, 66
    and urbanization, 73
    voting support, 72
  liberal, 64
    and urbanization, 73
    voting support, 72
de Vaca, Cabeza, 22
Downs, Anthony, 133n
Duckworth, Allen, 99n, 102n
Duke of Duval, 24
Dye, Thomas R., 10n, 27n, 130n

East Texas, as a political region, 47
Easton, David, 5n, 10n, 33n, 46n
Economic development in Texas, 31-32
Economic Opportunity Act, 92
Economic regions, 47-48
Economic regulation, 142-45
Edelman, Murray, 152n
Education, Texas
  among Mexican-Americans, 22
  and poverty, 89
  and voting behavior, 72
Eisenhower, Dwight, 73
Elazar, Daniel J., 41n, 46n, 50n, 51n
Elections, Texas
  campaigns, 95-97
  nonpartisan, 63-64, 131
  primary, 61-62
  voting alignments, 68-74
  voting participation, 65-74
  voting patterns, 1948-68, 71
  voting turnout, 66-68
Elitist democracy, 16
Environments, of political systems, 8-10
Environments, of Texas politics
  constitutional, 33-42
  socioeconomic, 19-33
Ericson, J. E., 36n
Establishment, Texas, 77, 81-83, 104
  component interests, 85
  and constitutional development, 104-5
  and local politics, 84-85
  and pressure groups, 83-84
Ethnic minorities, Texas, 20-27
Eulau, Heinz, 102n, 122n
Ewing, Cortez A. M., 112n
Executive Budget Office, 136
Executive department, Texas, 38
  and conversion process, 108
  independence, 94
  powers, in 1876 Constitution, 37

Farm Bureau, 28, 102

Farmers Union, 28
Federalism, and political systems, 5, 38-41, 139-40
Feedback, in conversion process, 14
Ferguson, Leroy C., 102n, 122n
Fesler, James W., 137n
Fragmentation, in political systems, 9, 14, 38-41, 150
Froman, Lewis A., Jr., 36n, 93n

Gantt, Fred Jr., 35n, 109n, 110n, 111n, 115n, 118n
Gatekeepers, as role participants, 6
German-Texans, 20, 26-27, 65
*Gibbons* v. *Ogden*, 39
Goals, as requisites of social systems, 3
Goldwater, Barry, 73
Gonzalez, Henry B., 24
Governor, Texas, 109-18
  appointive powers, 95, 110-111
  budget authority, 112-13, 136
  characteristics, 115
  and conversion process, 108
  and economic interests, 117
  executive authority, 110-12
  legislative authority, 112-14
  office appropriations, 138
  official messages, 112-13
  as party leader, 115-16
  personal style, 115-18
  removal powers, 111
  as role player, 109-18
  and special sessions, 112-14
  staff, 117-18
  term, 110
  veto power, 112, 114-15
  visibility, 128
Greenstein, Fred I., 48n
Groce, Jared E., 25
Gross, Bertram M., 141n
Grunbaum, Werner, 36n, 50n
Gulf Coastal Plain, as a region, 47

Hagard, Luther Jr., 35n, 109n
Henderson, Bancroft C., 131n
Highsaw, Robert B., 112n
Highway Commission, Texas, 94
Hofferbert, Richard I., 10n, 32n, 152n
Hogg, James, 38, 118
Holloway, Harry, 24n, 26n, 28n, 64n, 66n
House of Representatives, Texas, 78, 138.
  *See also* Legislature, Texas
Hyde Agency, 96

Ideology in Texas, 30, 40, 64
Image campaigns, 63
Immigrants, in Texas, 20

## Index

Individualism, as anti-union orientation, 30
Industrialization, Texas, 27, 29-30
Initiation, policy, 14, 109
Inputs, political, 4, 6, 8, 107, 133, 149
  as demands, 10-11, 77-105
  as supports, 11-12, 45-75
Integration, as requisite of social system, 4
Interest groups, and political demands, 77-105
  attitudes toward, 79
  comparative, 78-81
  defer-and-demand politics, 83
  *defined*, 78
  economic, 79, 82, 85
  and election campaigns, 95-97
  and privilege, 93-95
  strength, 79, 80 (table)
Issues, legislative, 53

Jacob, Herbert, 7n, 13n, 56n, 65n, 79n, 112n
Jewell, Malcolm E., 98n, 101n, 125n
Judiciary, Texas, 130-31
  budget, 138
  structure, 130
  terms, 131
Justice of the Peace, 130

Kaplan, Abraham, 3n
Kaplan, Chamberlain, 96
Kaplan, Morton A., 5n
Kennamer, Lorrin G., 22n, 25n, 29n
Key, V. O., Jr., 30n, 63, 63n
Kuvlesky, William P., 86n

Land Commissioner, Texas, 151
League of United Latin American Citizens (LULAC), 24
Legislation, bills (table), 126
Legislative Budget Board, 121-22, 136, 137, 138
Legislative Council, 138
Legislative Reference Library, 138
Legislators
  bargaining, 126-27
  career types, 123
  characteristics, 97-98, 122
  and lobbyists, 100-101
  as role participants, 122-23
  styles, 102
  tenure and turnover, 124
  terms, 119
  visibility, 128
Legislature, Texas, 84, 118-28
  amateurism, 103
  committee action, 123-27
  committees, 121
  and constitutional restraints, 120
  and conversion process, 108
  functions, 119
  issues, 53
  leadership, 120-22
  organization, 120-22
  oversight, 127-28
  quorum, 120
  rules and privileges, 119-20
  seniority system, 124, 127
  sessions, 113-14
  size, 119
  system character, 118-19
  tenure and turnover, 103
Lerner, Max, 1n
Lever, Michael F., 86n, 90n
Liberalism, Texas, 30
Lieutenant Governor, Texas, 108, 120, 121, 124, 136
Light Crust Doughboys, 116
Lineberry, Robert L., 58n
Lipsky, Michael, 13n
Liquor Control Board, 129
Lobbying, 97-103
  comparative data, 97
  definition, 97
  effects, 102-3
  number of registered lobbyists, 83, 98
  as a profession, 99
  regulation, 103
  styles, 101
Lobbyists
  characteristics, 97-98
  and legislators, 100-101
  number, 98-99
  registration, 78
  self-starters vs. drifters, 98
Local government, in Texas, 41, 85-86
Lockard, Duane, 36n
Locke, John, 37, 40
Lowi, Theodore J., 134n

McClendon, Gordon, 73
McCleskey, Clifton, 24n, 26n, 28n, 64n, 66n, 68n
McCrone, Donald J., 27n
McLemore, S. Dale, 22n
Malec-Ready, 96
Mansfield, Michael, 63n
Martin, Roscoe C., 41n
Mayo, Henry B., 15n
Merrill, Bruce, 68n
Mexican War, 22
Mexican-Americans, Texas, 20-21, 22-24, 149, 151
  education, 22-23
  employment, 23

## 164   Index

judicial treatment, 131
militancy, 153
and party factionalism, 65
poverty, 86-92
regional concentrations, 48
voting rates, 68
Michel, Jerry B., 102n
Migrants, role in Texas, 20
Milbrath, Lester W., 65n, 67n
Miller, Warren E., 69n
Mills, C. Wright, 16n
Mitchell, Joyce, 133n
Mitchell, William C., 3n, 5n, 11n, 15n, 133n
Mosher, Frederick C., 141n
Murray, Richard W., 59n
Mutcher, Gus, 121

National Municipal League, 135
Negroes, Texas. See Black Texans
Nevin, David, 47n, 53n, 82n, 84n, 146n
Nimmo, Dan, 66n
North Texas, as a region, 47

O'Daniel, W. Lee, 111, 116, 117
Oden, William E., 103n, 122n, 123n
Olson, David M., 62n, 63n, 66n
Outputs, political, 4, 6, 8, 12-13, 45, 107-47, 149
  by administrative agencies, 13
  benefits, 12
  deprivations, 12
  distributive, redistributive, and regulatory, 134-35
  and outcomes, 12
Oversight, legislative, 127-28

Panhandle Texas, as a region, 47, 50
Parsons, Talcott, 3n
Participatory democracy, 15
Patrons, in Texas culture, 23-24
Patterson, Samuel C., 50n, 98n, 101n
Penniman, Clara, 141n
Permanent Council, 34
Pluralist democracy, 16
Political Association of Spanish-speaking Organizations (PASO), 24, 96
Political authorities, 36-38
  constitutional fragmentation, 14
  types, 5
Political community, in Texas, 33-34
Political culture
  attitudes, 46
  citizen vs. subject, 74-75
  *defined*, 9
  and discrimination, 90-91
  diversity, 10
  partisan factions, 63

and regionalism, 46
traditionalistic, individualistic, and moralistic types, 50, 51, 54, 63, 67, 74, 104, 112, 150
and voter turnout, 67
Political parties, 54-65, 74
  competition, 54, 56
  conventions, 60
  definition, 54
  factions, 63-65
  membership, 58
  nominations, 61-62
  numbers, 54
  organizations, 54, 58-60, 61
  partisan identifications, 58
  and party systems, 54-56
  and primaries, 61-62
  voting alignments, 68-74
Political processes, types
  conversions, 13-14
  inputs, 10-12
  outputs, 12-13
Political regime, 45-46
  attitudes toward, 146-47
  characteristics in Texas, 74
  and Constitution of 1876, 37-38
  in Texas history, 34-36
  values, 36, 135, 147
Political style, 9, 23-24
Political system
  changes in Texas, 152-54
  character, 1-18, 149
  conversion processes, 107-47
  definition, 5
  democratic, 2, 15-17
  environments, 6-10, 19-41
  inputs, 4-6, 77-105
  levels, 17
  outputs, 107-47
  synonymous with polity, 4
Polity. See Political system
Poll tax, in Texas, 24
Population, Texas growth, 28
Poverty, Texas, 86-92
  age and sex differences, 89-90
  black vs. white (table), 87
  and discrimination, 90-91
  and education, 89
  family composition, 89-90
  occupational differences, 88
  and residence, 87
  and voting rates, 68
PPBS, 141-42
Pressure system
  *defined*, 78
  groups, 78, 83
  and privilege, 83-85

*Index* 165

scope, 83
types, 80
Protestant Ethic, 143
Public relations, and elections, 96

Race-ethnicity, and voting, 70-74
Racial integration, attitudes (table), 91-92
Railroad Commission, Texas, 94, 121, 145
Ranney, Austin, 56n
Ransome, Coleman, 118n
RAZA ("La Raza Unida"), 24
Read-Poland Agency, 96
Reese, James, 25n, 29n
Regionalism, Texas, 46-50, 64
Registration, periodic vs. permanent, 66
Representatives Wives Club, 99
Republican, form of government, 15
Republican party, Texas, 40, 56, 153
　fragmentation, 61, 64
　Germanic attachments, 26
　and governorship, 116
　identifiers, 58
　and urbanization, 28, 73
　voting support, 70-71
Residence
　and poverty, 87
　and voting requirements, 66
*Reynolds* v. *Sims*, 40n
Richardson, Rupert Norvel, 25n
Riesman, David, 83n
Right to work laws, 144
Riker, William H., 133n
Rives, Dyke and Company, 96
Robinson, James A., 138n, 144n
Role participants, in system, 6, 108
　administrative, 128-29
　gubernatorial, 109-18
　judicial, 130-31
　legislative, 118-28
Rominger Agency, 96
Rubel, Arthur J., 99n

Schattschneider, E. E., 82n
Schick, Allen, 141n
Schlesinger, Joseph A., 37n, 112n
Schnabel, Charles A., 126n
Secretary of State, Texas, 108, 129, 143
Segregation, Texas attitudes, 50
Seligman, Lester, 62n
Senate, Texas
　operating appropriations, 138
　senatorial courtesy, 110
　*See also* Legislature, Texas
Sharkansky, Ira, 10n, 27n, 32n, 137n
Sheinburg, Sheila D., 102n
Shevky, Eshref, 70n
Shivers, Allan, 38, 109, 109n, 116, 117

Shrabanek, R. L., 48n
Sinclair, T. C., 36n, 131n
Slavery, in Texas, 25
Smith, Dick, 35n, 94n
Smith, Preston, 36, 70, 109, 114, 116, 151
Social class, Texas patterns, 48, 69-74
Social environments, of political systems, 8, 19-27
Social systems, requisites, 3-6
Sorauf, Frank, 122n
Soukup, James R., 24n, 26n, 28n, 64n
South Texas, as a region, 47
Spanish influence in Texas, 22-23
Spanish surname population, 20, 22, 23
Speaker, Texas House of Representatives, 121
　committee appointments, 124
　election, 124
Standpatter, as gubernatorial role, 109
State Affairs Committee, Texas, Senate, 136
State Auditor, Texas, 113, 138
State Banking Board, Texas, 145
State Board of Barber Examiners, Texas, 129
State Board of Controls, Texas, 113
State Board of Dental Examiners, Texas, 129
State Board of Education, Texas, 94
State Board of Hairdressers and Cosmotologists, Texas, 129
State Building Fund, 137
States, as political systems, 5-6
Stokes, Donald E., 69n
Supports, political
　political culture, 46-54
　political participation, 65-74
　political parties, 54-65
Supreme Court of Texas, 130
Systems analysis, defined, 2-3

Tax Board, 129
Taxes
　chain store, 144
　on gross receipts and production, 140
　on highway motor fuel, 140
　income, 139-51
　poll, 24
　property, 140
　regressive vs. progressive, 140
　sales, 78, 84, 140
Teacher Retirement Fund, 137
Terrell Election Law, 58, 96
Texas Apartment Association, 83
Texas Bill of Rights, 37
Texas College Student Loan Bonds, 137
Texas Declaration of Independence, 34, 37

## 166  Index

Texas League of Women Voters, 83
Texas Manufacturers Association, 99, 102
Texas Medical Association, 102
Texas Motor Transportation
   Association, 102
Texas Municipal League, 102
Texas State Board of Medical
   Examiners, 129
Texas State Building and Construction
   Trade Council, 83
Texas State Teachers Association, 83, 84
Texas War of Independence, 22, 34
The Texas Poll, 53n, 92n, 146, 146n, 147n
Thomas, A. J., Jr., 132n
Thomas, Ann Van Wynen, 132n
*Thomas* v. *Collins*, 143
Thometz, Carol Estes, 84n
Tower, John, 56
Trans-Pecos, as a region, 47, 50
Treasurer, Texas, 108, 113
Truman, David B., 16n, 78n, 92n
Tullock, Gordon, 133n
Tunnell, Byron, 121
Turman, James, 125

Unionization in Texas, 29-30, 143
University of Texas Board of Regents, 129
Upham, W. Kennedy, 86n, 90n
Urbanization in Texas, 27-28
   and political parties, 56, 65, 73
   and poverty, 88
   and voting alignments, 70-74

Verba, Sidney, 75n
Veteran Land Fund, 137
Vigness, David, 35n
Vines, Kenneth N., 56n, 65n, 79n, 112n
Voting behavior
   alignments, 68-74
   comparative turnout rates, 67
   legal qualifications, 66
   sociodemographic patterns, 69-74
   *See also* Elections, Texas

Wahlke, John C., 102n, 122n, 123n
Walker, Jack L., 32n
Wallace, Ernest, 35n
Weeks, O. Douglas, 132n
West Texas, as a region, 47
Wholesale Beer Distributors of Texas, 83
Wilbern, York, 137n
Wildavsky, Aaron, 135n
Wiseman, H. V., 5n
Wolfinger, Raymond E., 48n
Wright, David E., 86n
Wyner, Alan J., 111n
Yarborough, Don, 70
Yarborough, Ralph, 73

Zeigler, Harmon, 69n, 78n, 79n, 86n, 97n,
   98n, 101n, 122n
Zeller, Belle, 79n, 80n

JK
4825
1971
.N53

JK
4825

1971
.N53